PARENTING:
ONE CHANCE TO DO IT RIGHT

PARENTING:
ONE CHANCE TO DO IT RIGHT

E. ALLEN GRIFFITH

Faithful Life Publishers
North Fort Myers, Florida

ISBN-10: 0-9749836-3-2
ISBN-13: 978-0-9749836-3-9

Published by Faithful Life Publishers
3335 Galaxy Way, North Fort Myers FL 33903

Cover photo: www.istockphoto.com

Scripture quotations are from the Authorized King James Version of the Holy Bible.

Printed in the United States of America
16 15 14 13 12 11 10 09 08 07   1 2 3 4 5

This book is dedicated to our five children:
Jeffrey, Craig, Jennifer, Amy, and Kimberly.

Each one is a continuing source of blessing, love, and encouragement.
They have endured our parental strengths and weaknesses
and by God's grace have grown up to love and serve the Lord.
We pray God will graciously bless them in the rearing
of their children as He blessed us with each of them.
To each one I can say, I am so glad God gave you to me!

TABLE OF CONTENTS

PREFACE

The Lord has afforded me many blessings in marriage, family, and ministry. I can say without hesitation that there is no one on the face of this earth with whom I would want to trade places. Among those blessings, few (if any) could measure up to the privilege of being a dad.

Having grown up in a broken home, I longed for a dad at times and determined that if I ever had the chance I would seek to be the best dad I could be. Without question I have failed many times in achieving that goal, but the honor of having children has been one of my greatest joys in life.

Blessings have increased as my children have grown up with a love for the Lord, for my wife (Patricia) and me, and for each other. And those blessings have multiplied with a growing number of grandchildren enlarging the Griffith clan.

I recognize that many things I now teach concerning parenting were not fully thought out in our own parenting experience. A measure of trial and error existed in our home life. We did our best as we studied Scripture and had the opportunity to sit under various teachers and preachers who addressed marriage and family issues. Gradually, our understanding grew, and the more we learned, the more we were blessed by using Bible truth to develop our parenting philosophy and to improve our parenting skills. We are still learning as we watch our children rearing our grandchildren.

I have a heavy burden for families because I know the Word of God is true—but many are somewhat willingly ignorant of what the Bible says about families in general, and the rearing of children in particular. In too many homes Christianity is professed, but children grow up to choose the way of the world—and we might fear that many are growing up without a saving knowledge of the Lord Jesus Christ. I have often said that I could never accept the possibility that one of my children would grow up and not come to Christ. I am grateful for their testimony for the Lord, and I prayerfully expect that someday we will gather together in His presence. Now my burden has deepened as precious grandchildren have been entrusted to our children for the blessing of their homes. I again cannot fathom the possibility that one of them will refuse the Savior and choose the world.

We can take nothing of this world to heaven, but when we are saved we are not of the world. May each of us who are parents and grandparents enter fully into that spiritual warfare—where we will do the parental tasks divinely assigned to us according to God's Word and plead daily for the souls of our loved ones before the throne of God's grace.

INTRODUCTION

It is an amazing fact that in God's Word He has not only given us great truths to reveal Himself and unfold His eternal plan, but has also given us incredible detail on how to live our earthly life one day at a time and even one experience at a time. He tells us about the rebellion of Lucifer and the fall of many angels. He tells us the glories of the Cross and the resurrection of the Lord Jesus. Yet woven through the message of these deep truths are the practical teachings of how to be a good dad and mom to children who are entrusted to us as gifts from the God of heaven. Only as we know and believe the redemptive truths that thrill our soul in salvation are we ready to claim the practical truths that can build a life and testimony for Christ in our homes. It may seem unfair to some readers of this book, but unless you have received Jesus Christ as your personal Savior and are sure of a heavenly home when this life is over, you can never be the parent God wants you to be and the parent your children need you to be.

This book is addressed primarily to Christian parents who are willing to accept biblical teaching on parenting with the same conviction they accept biblical teaching on salvation. *Parenting: One Chance To Do It Right* is written with the firm conviction that the Bible teaches us how to properly rear the children God gives us and that carefully following scriptural admonition, warning, and instruction will give us every hope that our children can grow up to love and serve the Lord.

Of course, the text is not exhaustive, but gives a firm biblical foundation for child rearing, on which parents can rely and build upon to successfully raise their own children in spite of the unique personality, interests, abilities, and needs of the individual young person.

It is hoped that every parent will be motivated to search more deeply and fervently into God's Word to learn what can be learned about caring for that special treasure of a child God has given.

This book may be used for personal study or as a text for Sunday Schools or other Bible study settings.

1 PARENTAL RESPONSIBILITY

Is it possible in today's world to see children grow up to love the Lord and desire to serve Him? Can the corrupting forces of this world be overcome in the Christian home? Can a couple rear six or seven children and have good reason to trust that each and every one of them will receive Christ as Savior and then live a surrendered life?

Not only is it possible for such blessings to come to a Christian home, but sufficient scriptural encouragement exists to expect those things to occur. How can we express such hope, considering the times we are facing in this generation? Because, aside from the obvious need of God's grace, the greatest factor in determining how children turn out is the degree to which parents accept and carry out their God-given responsibilities. If such is not the case, parents are at the mercy of their environment and today's environment offers little hope for children.

We should affirm immediately that parental responsibility is not a curse, it is a blessing. It is not a curse for scripture to lay upon parents great responsibility for how their children turn out. It is a blessing that should drive us to the Bible for guidance in finding out how to rear our children for the glory of God. If parents will get serious about parenting, amazing results can be achieved. If parents will find out what God's Word says about family life and put it into practice, they would be thrilled at the emotional development and spiritual victories that are attained in the lives of their children. Parenting is not an easy task, but it is surely one of the most important and can be one of the most rewarding tasks assigned to us in the Word of God.

As a pastor for over 26 years at the same church, I carefully observed people rearing their children. Like it or not, results were predictable based on parenting patterns. For instance, the home I used to call *the father knows best home* consistently produced strong stable children. This was the home where dad was obviously the leader—where his life and testimony commanded the respect of his wife and children. Other homes, with equal consistency, produced children where one or more of them had obvious character flaws and spiritual weaknesses. Now it is readily admitted that these few words are an over-simplification of the situations, but let them for the moment illustrate that parenting and home life make an incredible difference in how children turn out.

To accept the message and challenge of this book, some are going to ask for an absolute guarantee that proper parenting will produce Christ-honoring children. They will note a child's old nature and his individual human will as obstacles to parental success. To be sure, these areas need to be considered.

At the same time, among those I have carefully observed over a period of years, I would be hard pressed to find an example of open rebellion among children whose parents followed the letter and spirit of the Word of God in its teachings on the family. Certainly no one can read another's heart. Therefore, we acknowledge that an outwardly obedient child may have a rebellious heart. But as the Scripture says in Proverbs 20:11, *"Even a child is known by his doings, whether his work be pure, and whether it be right."*

The point is simple. Contrary to the views of increasing numbers of people, the problem in the church is not that good parenting is incapable of producing good children. The problem today is that thousands upon thousands of parents, while attending good churches and often enrolling their children in good Christian schools, are weak in actual parenting.

It is interesting that while rejecting the worldly philosophy that *it takes a village to raise a child*, we have developed our own *Christian village* mentality—when our children go astray or collapse under today's pressures, we look for someone else to blame. One of the most common complaints among parents is that other Christians failed their children. The pastor did not care enough about the teens. The youth leader offered a poor program. The Christian school teacher was unfair or the administrator maintained rules and policies that were too strict. The fact is that any one or all of these complaints might be true in any given setting. However, these servants of the Lord are not the ones responsible for the spiritual and emotional well-being of young people. Parents are! If a family is blessed with a flawless team of church and school workers, it is a plus to be sure; but these laborers for Christ cannot be held accountable for young people who go the wrong direction.

On the other hand, if it is not failing Christian workers who are blamed, it is the increasing pressure coming from an ungodly world that serves as an excuse for rearing a generation which has little heart for God. Great temptations are set before our children through TV, videos, books, magazines, and dress styles, along with the availability of drugs, alcohol, and sensual things. They are literally bombarded with worldliness and the Devil's lies about "the good life." Parenting, though, is more than having our children in good places with good people to receive good instruction. Parenting involves the extremely difficult task of protecting our children from those people, places, and sources of information that will destroy them spiritually and morally. Let no one miss this emphasis. *This is parental responsibility!!!*

We cannot depend upon any element of a given community to do for our children the tasks divinely assigned to us. Let us face the fact that no one is going to clean up society apart from a genuine and extremely far-reaching Holy Spirit revival. The Apostle Paul said, *"...in the last days perilous time shall come"* (II Timothy 3:1). In other words, the world will continue down the pathway of sin and wickedness until our Lord comes.

If parenting is doomed to failure because *"evil men and seducers shall wax worse and worse, deceiving, and being deceived"* (II Timothy 3:13), then perhaps Christians should stop having children. Thankfully, successful parenting is not dependent on the world around us. The need of our day is for godly, devoted parents to commit themselves to rearing their children with strict adherence to the principles and instructions found in the Word of God. That commitment requires time and energy that few seem willing to invest in family life.

This chapter does not give details on parenting. It is designed to bring each parent to the point of facing parental obligation. Psalm 127:3 says, *"Lo, children are an heritage of the LORD and the fruit of the womb is his reward."* A parent must respond to those words with a humble acceptance of the awesome task of being a dad or mom. To do that involves taking responsibility for the child that the God of the Universe has given. While the Lord opens and closes the womb, it is parents who directly pass life on to the next generation. The soul of the child comes into being by the seed of the man joining with the ovum of the woman—then life immortal is conceived. Children enter into eternal existence upon conception. Parents must face the reality of what it takes in time, love, concern, prayer, instruction, discipline, and weeping to see their little one reject this sin cursed world and ready his soul for the world to come.

When a parent looks at his child, he must consider the following thoughts and words:

The Parent's Covenant: I Am Responsible

I am responsible. I cannot and will not blame anyone else if this child goes the wrong direction; and if he chooses the right path, I will give all the glory and praise to God. While others may forget to pray for him, I will pray for him everyday. When others fail him—and they will, I will be there to encourage him and help renew a right spiritual perspective in his life. When he falls, I will be there to lift him up and get him back on the right path. When he has trouble seeing what the Lord is doing in his life, I will be there to let him see Christ in me with words of assurance that Jesus never fails but always does things well. God allowed this child to begin his eternal existence in my family, in my care, in my arms. Under my roof he will find every reason to put his faith in the living Savior. He will be trained according to the principles of Scripture. Discipline will not be lacking, but love will be overflowing. And by God's grace, in that hour when we gather on the other side, my child will be with me as I fall at the feet of my Lord and enter into that Eternal Day.

Scripture is full of numerous passages that relate to parenting. Many of them give specific instructions. Others teach by way of principle and some simply record parenting experiences. Overall, an incredible amount of material in the Bible is about the family and the rearing of children. There are too many verses to quote in this text and really too many to even list; but as the Scriptures are read, studied, and used for meditation they will provide guidance, instruction, and hope for every serious parent. They will place tremendous obligation upon parents to rear their children correctly. They will clearly show that some parenting practices are right and some are wrong. They will help us face the fact that it is not enough to simply do our best—we must do our best according to the guidelines taught in Scripture.

Biblical Instruction and Hope for Parents

Train up a child in the way he should go: and when he is old,
he will not depart from it. Proverbs 22:6

A common question about this verse is whether it is a promise or a principle. The question has risen in this last generation because there is a genuine concern about many children of Christians and Christian workers who are going the wrong direction. Some, therefore, are advocating that we receive this verse as a principle, since it is found in the book of Proverbs; but they advocate caution in receiving it as a promise. While the issue could be debated, the fact is that—regardless of whether it is a principle or a promise— something is going wrong surrounding the practical application of this precious text. If children go astray, parents must conclude one of three things:

- God did not fulfill His promise;

- the principle does not work very well;

- they did not do a good job of training.

If, in fact, parents fail to train their children in accordance with the teachings of God's Word, it does not matter whether the verse in question is a promise or a principle.

Proverbs 22:6, however, was not given as a threat against or condemnation of failing parents. It was given to inspire hope—hope that thrives in a thoroughly Christ-honoring home where children are being effectively trained as outlined in Scripture. Parents need to be determined to learn all they can about child training from the Bible and prayerfully put it into practice. Whether the text is principle or promise is moot without implementation of the training. Take this verse as a foundation for hope in child rearing and build upon it.

At the same time, let's not be afraid as parents to acknowledge our failures. When some children go the way of the world, many dads and moms immediately defend themselves as having been excellent parents who could not possibly be held to any accountability for their children's flaws. The fact is, we all fail to one degree or another—so let's claim the grace that comes with humility and beg God to work in spite of us, instead of proudly declaring we have done no wrong. Humility is consoled by Divine grace; while pride is met by Divine resistance (James 4:6).

In parenting we need that grace as desperately as we need the hope offered by Proverbs 22:6. Believe this: as a promise or a principle the verse works when the training occurs.

One that ruleth well his own house, having his children
in subjection with all gravity. 1 Timothy 3:4

This text was given by Paul to Timothy as part of the criteria to be considered in the selection of a pastor. It is primarily a requirement regarding the character and conduct of the man—"*one that ruleth well...with all gravity.*" However, his character and conduct are to be reflected in the lives of his children. This verse is obviously acknowledging parental training as extremely important. It is to be assumed that if the children are not *"in subjection,"* the man is not suitable for pastoral service. That God requires the children of pastors to be under control, and that the pastor is to accomplish the task with all gravity, says that dad is responsible as a parent for how his child lives.

The phrase *"with all gravity"* means that dad's parenting skills are to inspire reverence and respect from his children, as he keeps them in subjection. It might be argued that a child's obedience could be purely external response to authority, and perhaps produced out of fear of punishment. However, when reverence and respect are produced, it becomes evident that proper parental influence produces more than just surface obedience. This text lets us know that as parents we can and, in fact, are expected to have a tremendous impact on our child's attitudes, as well as his actions.

I trust parents will find hope here. Dads and moms, along with their children, are not merely helpless victims in a wicked world. Pastors and their wives, as well as all other parents, must realize that children can be brought under control and be successfully trained to respect parental authority. The Lord would not make this a requirement for pastoral service if it was not possible. In the 1 Timothy 3 context, it is given as a bottom line requirement for pastoral service, but it is surely an ideal for every family. Children in Christian homes are to display reverence and respect for their parents—and the parents are to make it happen.

> *For I know him, that he will command his children and his household*
> *after him, and they shall keep the way of the LORD,*
> *to do justice and judgment… Genesis 18:19*

This powerful statement was made by the Lord regarding Abraham and the rearing of his children. This word of commendation acknowledged a two-fold responsibility in parenting. The Lord said Abraham would not only *"command"* his children, but would *"command his children…after him."* The Lord's words suggest that not only would Abraham tell his children what to do, but he would lead them by example and they would follow. The results would have them *"keep[ing] the way of the Lord."*

To *"keep the way of the Lord"* includes far more than external performance. The word *keep* speaks of hedging about, guarding, preserving, and observing. The word *way* refers to a trodden path. The Lord was acknowledging that because of Abraham's parental care, his children would have a deep regard for and commitment to the path of God. Further it is said that they would do justice and judgment. The term translated *justice* is most often translated righteousness in the Old Testament and speaks of moral virtue and right living. The term *judgment* means discretion and discernment. It suggests good sense and good decision making.

Here then is another text to give hope to parents. We have every reason to believe that our children can grow up keeping the way of the Lord, doing justice and judgment. Let no one rob us of this hope nor cause us to retreat from aiming at this high and lofty goal. This is exactly what we want for our children. We do not want children who simply do what is right; we want children on the battlefield, defending the faith and holding the line in a day of compromise. This can happen in your family.

And his father had not displeased him at any time in saying,
Why hast thou done so? I Kings 1:6

This interesting statement is made about Adonijah, the son of David. The previous verse tells us that Adonijah *"exalted himself saying, I will be king."* Then we are immediately informed that *"his father had not displeased him at any time in saying, Why hast thou done so?"* Can the implication be any clearer? This young man had been spoiled through permissiveness and finally rebelled against the authority of his father and king. The rebellion is directly attributed to the permissiveness. If David had disciplined his son properly, Adonijah would not have rebelled. Adonijah was the son of a king and was obviously very wealthy, but these privileges were not the cause of his rebellion. Parenting made the difference and, in this case, the results were tragic. Parents are not doomed to have rebellious children. It is the way children are reared that most greatly affects the way they turn out. We are encouraged to believe that if David had been different, Adonijah would have been different.

And, ye fathers, provoke not your children to wrath:
but bring them up in the nurture and admonition of the Lord. Ephesians 6:4

This very familiar verse tells fathers that they are not to provoke their children to wrath. The terms *provoke* and *wrath* are translated from the same term in the Greek language. It speaks of the wrath that comes from exasperation. Often children feel frustrated through parental temper, inconsistency, or hypocrisy.

Their response is wrath. They express rage and anger through words, attitudes, and actions. To be sure, a child may express anger and rage for other reasons, but there is a special warning here for parents. Proper nurture (training, instruction, and correction) and admonition (appropriate rebuke and warning, reaching the mind) will keep the child from reacting to and rejecting parental authority. While children are clearly told to obey their parents in all things— parents are reminded that how they handle their God-given authority will make a world of difference in how their children respond.

The verses on which we have commented are just a small representation of all there is on parenting in the Scriptures. These texts and many others that could have been selected demonstrate the divinely intended influence of parents on their children.

Other influences can be exerted on our children, of course—some being good and some being bad. Parents, who by their authority can limit and control all other influences, are to be the greatest influence. Friends, relatives, school, church, TV, reading material, daily schedules, and a host of other things that affect children can be indirectly (and often directly) overseen by dad and mom. The necessary oversight takes a great deal of time and effort—but it can be done.

What is a Parent to Do?

As already stated, this chapter does not give details on parenting. Later chapters will deal with some of the day-to-day challenges of rearing children. At the very outset of this book, however, there are some things that can and must be done by parents.

1. Accept responsibility for children

Whether it is a prayerful commitment to the Lord or simply a new beginning in attitude to reflect the thoughts of The Parent's Covenant, parents must see themselves as responsible for how their children grow up. Parents must face the seriousness of rearing a child and commit themselves to fulfilling the task with careful and dutiful adherence to the Scriptures. The commitment may involve a careful review of priorities to determine necessary changes that may be needed to allow the time, energy, and effort necessary to be successful. Let it be remembered that good parenting is not a matter of doing one's best—it is doing one's best in accordance with the teaching of Scripture.

2. Determine that you will blame no one else for your children's ways

Throughout my years of ministry I have seen scores of parents ignore or directly reject what the Bible says about the rearing of children. Too often when their children turn out the wrong way, they have looked for someone or something else to blame. Determine you will not do this. Many influences in your child's life will pressure him to think wrong and act wrong. Much of parenting is protection and much of it is positive training. Give yourself 100% to the task and determine that if all goes well you will give the glory to the Lord—but if things do not go well, you will not blame other people or the pernicious world in which we live. If parents face the fact that they can blame no one else, they will get more serious about the obligation associated with bringing a child into this world.

3. Begin daily prayer for children by name

"I'll pray for you" are words that come easy but may mean nothing. Realizing the need for the grace of God in salvation and surrender, parents must pray regularly for their children. If a parent does not care enough to pray for his own, would he be so foolish to believe someone else does? The Bible teaches that prayer makes a difference in life's events. Parents must believe prayer for their child will make a difference and they must pray.

4. Lower expectations for others

Parents should rejoice in the help and godly influence of other Christians upon their children, but must face the fact that others are only part of a support team. They may not be all a parent would want them to be and they may fail in their tasks, but a child must not be allowed to stand or fall based on the testimony or ministry of a pastor, youth leader, school teacher, administrator, or even relatives. Parents must be prepared to walk with their children through the difficult times when others fail them or seemingly treat them unfairly. The less we expect from others, the less our disappointment when they fail and the greater our joy and appreciation when they minister effectively.

5. Protect children from improper influences

Parents must not allow children to go certain places or do certain things because of the fear of offending other adults. Convictions must not be surrendered, especially when the parent compromises what he really believes. For example, the invitation for a child to spend the night at another home may have to be refused if it is known that the activities of the other home are going to undermine the teachings and stand of one's family. It may not be easy to explain to those who extend the invitation, but parents must not put their children into those situations of risk, even if the two sets of parents are friends. As mentioned elsewhere in this text, protection is a great part of parenting. Children should be kept as innocent as possible as long as possible.

6. Keep the home free of worldly influences

Parents will have a tough job overcoming external influences on their children and, therefore, must keep a wholesome atmosphere at home. The TV, videos, radio, reading material, music, pictures, posters, along with all else that enters the ear gate and the eye gate must be carefully guarded. Whatever "rights" a child may have will never include the one to pollute his mind and heart with this world's wickedness while he lives in a home where Christ is the head.

It is somewhat amazing that society is beginning, in many cases, to recognize parental responsibility. Laws are being enacted in various places holding parents accountable for young people who refuse to go to school. In other places parents can be fined if children violate community curfews or commit certain crimes. It's about time! It should not surprise us, however, that parents are still unable to control their children and things are generally getting worse. The reason things will continue to degenerate is because most people have rejected their only source of real hope, the Bible. It alone has the information needed to rear children successfully.

While society continues its downward spiral, the people of God should be shining as bright lights in a dark place. Believers should be telling a frustrated world to look at Christian families to see a demonstration of the power of the Gospel and the transforming work of the Living Word of God. Instead, children from Christian homes are being lost to the allurements of the world in record numbers. Even Christian colleges and seminaries report that virtually every freshman class manifests less spiritual maturity and spirituality then the one before. The answer is not to be found in the church or the school because these institutions are but a reflection of the homes from which young people come. The Lord's servants in places of ministry should strive for excellence and do their best to proclaim God's message. However, if hope exists for long term change, it is to be found in the establishment of godly families. Men and women must take the truth they hear in the pew or classroom and put it into practice at home. Christian people have all the resources necessary to enjoy a successful and happy home life. Claim it for yourself, with an open Bible, a tender heart, and dependence on the Spirit of God.

If your home is not really what you want it to be, or more importantly, not what God wants it to be, now is the time to make a difference. You may have to apologize for the past, but you cannot change it—so do not live with continual guilt over past failures. Confess sin to the Lord and, where appropriate, make things right with people. Next, prayerfully consider what should be different about your home and establish a plan to achieve those goals. Remember, not everyone in your family may be ready or even desire to change. You must work wisely to bring everyone along with you as you make adjustments in standards or practices. You may need to move very slowly to earn the respect of family members you have hurt in times past. Be aware that it is common for a parent to come under conviction that home life must change and then come on so strongly that he loses everybody along the way.

Begin by begging the Lord to change you. Let Him transform your thoughts, words, actions, and attitudes so family members can see that you are different before you announce your plans for change in your home. Move ahead with firm determination, but move slowly, prayerfully, and compassionately with your family. Get good counsel from your pastor, or another Christian worker, so you can have a broader perspective when making tough decisions or facing difficult situations. Study the Scriptures carefully to know how to respond to any circumstance you may face. Pray fervently, remembering you must do some things —while only God can do other things.

2 WHAT YOU ARE

O ther chapters of this book will discuss a variety of parenting skills and "how to" methods, but no chapter will be more important than this one. It has been years since I first heard this warning—what we are as Christians speaks so loudly that the world cannot hear what we say. If that challenge is appropriate as a testimony to the unsaved world, it is doubly important for us as parents. Our day-to-day life before our children will go a long way in determining what they will become as they grow into adulthood. DO NOT go on to another part of this book until you have thought carefully about the pages you are now reading.

Unfortunately, one of the excuses young people use for rejecting the way of the Lord is the hypocrisy they see in the lives of their parents. Those children should understand that, while the failures of their parents may seem to justify choosing the world over Christ, such reasoning will never stand up in the courts of heaven. At the same time, parents must face the fact that, while their sins can never be a child's legitimate excuse for rejecting the Savior, those same failures serve as the practical reasons why many young people go astray. Parents can try to promote the idea that when their children get older they are on their own, but sometimes that is just a cloak to hide a spiritually weak home life.

Too often children report that their parents act one way on Sunday (when other Christians are looking) but act quite differently at home during the rest of the week. These same parents are often found serving in a local church, by teaching a class or holding an office. While no one else may know it, their own children realize they are unworthy of those positions of spiritual testimony and leadership. We might fool the people at our church for a long time, because they usually see us at our best. On the other hand, our children see us in every situation. They watch us in the good times and the bad times. They observe us when all is well and they see us react under pressure. They hear our words, witness our actions, and observe our attitudes in every variety of circumstance we face. For a time little ones may be unaffected if our ways are sinful, but as they mature they will soon recognize us for what we really are.

The Scriptures let us know the importance of our example and that it must be genuine. Few words of greater condemnation are found in the Word of God than our Lord's rebuke of the Pharisees. In Matthew 23:27-28 Jesus said, *"Woe unto you, scribes and Pharisees, hypocrites! for ye are like unto whited sepulchres, which indeed appear beautiful outward, but are within full of dead men's bones, and of all uncleanness. Even so ye also outwardly appear righteous unto men, but within ye are full of hypocrisy and iniquity."* For application to the Christian parent, the *whited sepulcher* could be the public testimony at church or with friends, while the *dead men's bones and uncleanness* are the actions and attitudes which are manifested in the privacy of home.

The old adage "children are to be seen and not heard" could suggest that children are not to talk, they are to listen and observe. Be assured, every child is listening and observing, even if we think they sometimes talk too much. Therefore, no parent dare *appear* one way in front of others and then *be* different at home. It is a sure way to drive children from the Lord. Remember, your children are watching everything you do. No Christian parent can afford a pharisaical testimony before his children.

The Reality of Salvation

When someone truly gets saved, a dramatic change occurs in his life. That is not opinion—it is what the Bible says. In II Corinthians 5:17 Paul wrote, *"Therefore if any man be in Christ, he is a new creature* (creation)*: old things are passed away; behold, all things are become new."* How are we to understand this verse in light of other scriptural teaching?

The Bible does not teach the doctrine known as *eradication of the old nature*. When we are saved, we are still prone to sin and still capable of committing great wickedness. Galatians 5 warns us of what the flesh can produce if we fail to walk in the Spirit. At salvation, the old nature is not eradicated.

Likewise, the doctrine of *perfectionism* is not found in the Bible. There is no chance to achieve such a level of spiritual maturity that we will never sin again here on earth. Romans 8 tells us that as Christians we are predestined to be conformed to the image of Christ, but that will not be fulfilled until we see Him. Our perfection will come in heaven. We will never experience it here. As John wrote in I John 3:2, it is when our Lord Jesus Christ shall appear, that we shall be like Him.

The Bible does teach that when we are saved, we are newly born and need to grow (I Peter 2:2). We are subject to the possibility of failing to grow as rapidly as we should, and we may commit sin unworthy of our salvation. The Corinthian believers illustrated this well, as clearly seen in I Corinthians 3:1-3 where Paul addressed these problems. So let's face it—Christians do sin. Having said all these things, however, let's face the fact that when one gets saved his life dramatically changes. He is a new creature, born again, and indwelt by the Holy Spirit. II Corinthians 5:17 does not say old things *ought* to pass away or that they *ought* to become new—it says they **DO**. If we profess to be saved, the change ought to be evident in our thoughts, words, attitudes, and actions. As the song writer put it, *"Things are different now, something happened to me."*

In his first epistle, John gave appropriate evidences of true salvation that should manifest themselves in the believer. They included: keeping the Lord's commandments (2:3); not loving the world (2:15); not continuing sinful practice as a way of life (3:9); and loving the brethren (3:14). Salvation is new life! Among the most important people to witness that new life are those with whom we live every day.

Let us quickly make this point, however, especially to newly saved parents—we are not simply talking about a change in the standards of the home. The Bible calls for a change in the way we live and how we treat each other.

In too many homes dad and mom get saved and new rules are immediately established for TV, video tapes, dress, appearance, church attendance, friends, acceptable activities, etc., but the parents do not carry out the effects of their salvation with love, kindness, and compassion toward their children. Sometimes dad and mom are still harsh, unkind, unpleasant, and at times even vindictive, but now they act that way in the name of their newly found faith. Christianity changes the person, and then the person is to let the inward change reflect in his outward life. Paul said in Galatians 5:25, *"If we live in the Spirit, let us also walk in the Spirit."*

Now lest someone misunderstand, it is not that new standards are inappropriate. In the home of the newly saved, they are no doubt imperative. The point is that parents must let their salvation be obvious by the way they talk and act and not simply by the establishment of new rules. The life of the parent should be characterized by love, joy, peace, and other qualities that can be manifested in the Spirit-filled Christian. These traits demonstrate the reality of salvation. The first challenge of good parenting is to live a solid Christian testimony in front of our children.

A dad contacted me for counsel regarding his children. They would not obey him and, in fact, would outright defy him. What was he to do? I visited the home and eventually spent time with them all. Everyone saw the real problem, but dad. His children grew up under incredibly strict standards of dress and practice; but they had a dad who (while requiring adherence to the rules) lost his temper, abused his family in various ways, and used ungodly language. His use of Ephesians 6:1 *"Children, obey your parents"* was a mockery of God's Holy Word. The children had learned to use the Scriptures for their own convenience. They could quote all the Scriptures related to poor parenting and the justification of disobedience to ungodly authority. Was it okay for the children to disobey? No. Was it realistic for their father to expect them to obey? No. My counsel to the children was that their father's failure could never justify their sin of rebellion. At the same time, their dad had to face his hypocrisy, if any real change was going to take place in the home.

Day-to-Day Example

The parent who knows the Lord should demonstrate how to live the Christian life by the way he handles his day-to-day experiences. Read and consider the following Old Testament challenge. It was given by Moses to show parents how to make sure their children did not forget God. As you read the passage you will notice that the way they carried out their parenting would be a determining factor in how their children turned out. Let me emphasize that point again. As you read the passage you will notice that the way parents carried out their parenting would be a determining factor in how their children turned out. This is true for all of us.

> *Deuteronomy 6:1-5 — "Now these are the commandments, the statutes, and the judgments, which the LORD your God commanded to teach you, that ye might do them in the land whither ye go to possess it: That thou mightest fear the LORD thy God, to keep all his statutes and his commandments, which I command thee, thou, and thy son, and thy son's son, all the days of thy life; and that thy days may be prolonged. Hear therefore, O Israel, and observe to do it; that it may be well with thee, and that ye may increase mightily, as the LORD God of thy fathers hath promised thee, in the land that floweth with milk and honey. Hear,*

O Israel: The LORD our God is one LORD: And thou shalt love the LORD thy God with all thine heart, and with all thy soul, and with all thy might."

This clear word of instruction from Moses to the parents of Israel still holds tremendous importance for us. Let's consider its message...

Moses told the adult generation of his day that the commandments, statutes, and judgments of God were *"commanded...that ye might do them."* In other words, parenting was to begin by example. Still today parents are to obey the Word of God and their children should be able to observe them doing it.

Let me give a single illustration from the New Testament. Philippians 2:14 says, *"Do all things without murmurings and disputings."* This isolated instruction is one of scores found in Scripture for the New Testament believer. As parents, how do we respond to this commandment? If we do not obey it in respect to our responsibilities, why should we expect our children to obey it? How often do children see moms and dads murmuring and disputing about their obligations?

Parents who want to rear godly children will have to make a conscientious effort to obey the Bible in the daily affairs of life. It is not enough to say we believe the Bible or adhere to a strict doctrinal statement. We must apply biblical instruction and principle to every situation we face. Whether it is how we handle a matter on the job, a difficulty with a neighbor, or a flat tire on the car, we must display obedience to the detailed instructions of Scripture. If we do not fulfill our obligations without murmuring and disputing, how dare we expect it from our children. If we profess to be Bible-believing Christians, but limit that profession to acceptance of the biblical record of history, doctrine, and prophecy, we have failed. We must adhere to the detailed admonitions of Scripture. It is in this area that we establish our testimony before the world and our own family. This cannot be emphasized too much. Whether in our daily routine or in a time of testing, we must run to the Scriptures to find out what they teach as appropriate action in a given situation—and then we must do it. Our children need to know that we genuinely live by the Bible. To profess to believe the Bible and refuse to specifically live by the Bible is a terrible form of hypocrisy.

Moses went on to say that we are to *"fear the LORD."* Someone has defined the *fear of the Lord* as the "wholesome dread of displeasing God." It is not to live in continual fright of God, but to be ashamed before Him for our sinful ways, knowing that we are answerable to Him according to His standards of holiness. Though it is a trite illustration, I liken the fear of the Lord to a little boy who has been bad all day for his mother and now it is time for dad to arrive home. The dread he feels in waiting to see his dad is real, but the dread is wholesome. Would your children testify that you fear God? Would they attest that you do not worry what people think about you, but you intensely strive for Divine acceptance? If our children do not see the fear of the Lord in us, should we expect them to reverence Him?

So many people are concerned about their right to express themselves in their own way or live to the fullest extent of Christian liberty that they forget we serve a holy God, who is jealous for our complete surrender and utmost devotion. Will anyone be chided at the Judgment Seat of Christ for having sought to live too closely to Him while on earth? Solomon said, *"Be not wise in thine own eyes: fear the LORD, and depart from evil"* (Proverbs 3:7). Do our children see in us an abhorrence of sin?

While fearing the Lord, we are encouraged to not fear men. Psalm 56:4 says, *"… in God I have put my trust; I will not fear what flesh can do unto me."* Men pleasers are not held in high esteem by the Lord. John 12:43 records the cowardly response of the chief rulers of Israel during the earthly life of Christ. They refused to confess Him openly because they loved the praise of men more than the praise of God. How often in Christian homes standards are set or practices carried out because believers are worried what men may think, instead of caring only about what matters to God. Would we be so foolish as to believe our children do not notice?

In a number of places, the Bible warns us against these things. Now we certainly should avoid offending others whenever possible. When Paul cautioned the believers at Colosse, he said we are to serve in *"singleness of heart, fearing God"* (Colossians 3:22). Our children must not view us as people who are always waiting to see what the crowd is going to do. Parents must be willing to stand alone for righteousness, if they hope for their children to do the same. Our plans, goals, and decisions should be governed by the desire to please the Lord. Our children should be able to witness our consecration to His will and His way without regard for the approval of men.

Through my years of ministry, I have always been amazed at people who make comments to others like "We don't do that at our church." I have always wondered how they viewed their responsibilities in determining how to serve the Lord. As a parent, I do not want my children to think that our church is setting the standards of our home, nor is any other individual having that kind of influence. I want our children to know that we have sought the Lord through His Word and prayer to discern what is best for our family. Our standards may not be as strict as some or stricter than others, but hopefully they are biblically based and honoring to our Savior.

We have already noted that our children will be quick to recognize the hypocrisy of a mere outward show of spirituality. A genuine heart for God will be expressed through visible efforts to give Him our best. Most would agree that today's Christianity is lived on the basis of convenience rather than conviction. For instance, the average church has a relatively large percentage of its constituency attend on Sunday morning. On Sunday night that number will be cut in half and at the midweek service will be cut in half again. For special meetings few will be faithful. Workers are generally in short supply, resulting in 10% of the people doing 90% of the work. Do these statistics manifest the fear of the Lord among the people of God? Where do you fit in? Is service for Christ in your life marked by conviction or is it a matter of convenience?

In our Deuteronomy passage (vs. 5) Moses then added these thoughts: We are to love God with all our heart, soul, and might. Think what it means to love God. It has little to do with emotion. So much of Christianity today is about feelings that we often miss spiritual truth. Foundational to biblical love is sacrifice. If we love God, it will be evidenced in sacrifice, not necessarily in feelings. God so loved the world that He gave (sacrificed) His Son (John 3:16). Christ so loved the church that He gave (sacrificed) Himself (Ephesians 5:25). We should evaluate our love for God by the sacrifices we make to serve and honor Him.

Sadly, the Lord seems to get people's leftovers, instead of the sacrificial first fruits. For instance, many churches offer Saturday evening worship, so people can have Sunday for leisure. Even some churches that would designate themselves as Bible believing are known to cancel evening services for the summer or do away with midweek prayer. Malachi rebuked the people of Israel because they spoke of their service for God by saying, *"Behold, what a weariness is it!"* Attending services often becomes a matter of debate in the Christian home. Dad has work to do that he brought home from the office and mom is tired; so until an hour before the evening service, no one is sure who is going to church. Can you imagine anyone getting up on Monday morning and debating whether or not they are going to work? Hardly!

Worldly obligations are accepted and, for the most part, faithfully fulfilled. Fulfilling spiritual duty seems to be viewed as optional. Someone might ask,

"Is it not hypocritical to go to church when you do not feel like it?" The answer to that is no! It is never hypocritical to fulfill your duty or meet an obligation, even if you do not feel like it. We will get more out of church by attending through desire, but we should attend whether we feel like it or not. The Lord ordained the church as His place of fellowship, feeding, and service. Parents should be in church and their children should see it as a priority in their family.

How about sacrificial giving? If tithing is practiced, it must be recognized that *"the tithe…is the LORD'S: it is holy unto the LORD"* (Leviticus 27:30). If the tithe is already His, what do we do sacrificially to show Him our love? Do our children ever see us SACRIFICE for God?

Another challenge about love in the Bible is a warning found in I John 2:15— *"love not the world."* Here, again, love will be evidenced in sacrifice. In Matthew 6:19-21 the Lord Jesus said, *"Lay not up for yourselves treasures upon earth, where moth and rust doth corrupt, and where thieves break through and steal: But lay up for yourselves treasures in heaven, where neither moth nor rust doth corrupt, and where thieves do not break through nor steal: For where your treasure is, there will your heart be also."*

Have you ever considered that every day we take a small portion of our earthly existence and invest it in some way? As the Lord Jesus put it, we lay up treasure. We use up a little segment of life, sacrificing it for some purpose. One day at a time passes into history, never to be reused, never to be regained. Are we building heavenly treasure or earthly treasure? What did you do today? Did you sacrifice today's precious moments for worldly endeavors, attempting to achieve mere temporal goals? Or far better, did your day and its activities count for eternity? If you are not sure, you might ask your children to see how they view the things that take your time and energies.

We sacrifice for the things that are important to us. You might be asked to go somewhere or make some purchase. If those things are not important to you, you might quickly respond by pleading that you have neither time nor money to fulfill the request. On the other hand, if it is a place you really want to go or an item you really desire to have, you might very well make whatever sacrifice is necessary to achieve the desired end. If our children witness in us a sacrificial love for earthly things and little sacrifice for the Lord, there is not much hope they will develop a true love for Him in their own lives.

Notice the purpose of Moses' admonitions (vs. 2-3). He said his words were for the parent and his son and his son's son that their days would be prolonged, that it would be *"well"* with them, and that they could increase mightily. These encouragements had particular significance to the Israelites as they moved toward the Promised Land, but there is great application for us. Unfortunately, it is not *"well"* with many Christian families today. Too often an observer would be hard pressed to identify real differences between the daily activities, attitudes, and atmosphere of the Christian home and the non-Christian home. Many Christian homes are falling apart and families are not *"increasing mightily."*

God's plan is for a couple to produce a godly heritage of many generations who will live for Him and carry forth the testimony of Christ. Too many families produce young people who are nominal Christians at best and sometimes are outright rebels against God. It must not be that way in your home. Your day-to-day example is extremely important. As your children watch you every-day—what do they see?

An Invitation to Trust

Think with me of another important Scriptural text for parents. In Proverbs 23:26 we read, *"My son, give me thine heart, and let thine eyes observe my ways."* This is a solemn invitation. When a parent says, *"Give me thine heart,"* he is saying, *"You can trust me, I will be there for you."* The added words *"let thine eyes observe my ways"* mean *"I will show you how to live."* This is parenting at its best. Children need the security that comes from a parent being present and active in their lives and being worthy of their trust.

Can we dare invite our children to let their eyes observe our ways? *"Don't look at me, look at Christ"* has been a cheap way for many to excuse their irresponsibility. No doubt we will fail our children from time to time, but if they are to *look at Christ* they must be able to see Him in us. When we fail them, we must apologize, make things right, and seek again to magnify the Savior through our lives.

How will our children learn to live if they cannot learn by watching us? Can we display fits of temper and think our children will not throw their toys? Can we raise our voices in anger and think our children will control their tongues? Can we live in bitterness toward others and think our children will forgive those who sin against them? Will we produce children who are sold out to Christ, if they observe our ways? What if our children turn out just like us? Will God approve? Will others like them? Will we like them?

Proverbs 20:7 states, *"The just man walketh in his integrity: his children are blessed after him."* Here is a text filled with hope for the faithful man. His life is a pattern, established for his offspring to follow. The blessings of his integrity will fall upon his children. This is not some mystical work of grace. It is the result of the practical training of children that comes from observing a parent, especially a dad who lives a life of integrity in all his ways.

Proverbs 17:6b says, *"The glory of children are their fathers."* Here is yet another text filled with hope for the godly dad. Built into a child's heart is the tendency to glory or boast in his dad. Dad is put on a pedestal of honor and respect. The danger is that he may fall off the pedestal by failing to parent in accordance with the full teaching of Scripture. The hope is that the young child will follow his dad all the way to the foot of the cross—there to meet the Savior and consecrate all to Him.

Reality Will Bring Respect

To complete our thinking about *what we are* as being critical to successful parenting, consider one more important text. In 1 Timothy 4:12 Paul wrote, *"Let no man despise thy youth; but be thou an example of the believers, in word, in conversation, in charity, in spirit, in faith, in purity."* Paul's challenge to Timothy was this—do not let anyone ignore you, hold you in contempt, or look down on you because you are young. Overcome that seeming hindrance to effective ministry by exhibiting a solid, undeniable example in six areas: word, conversation, charity, spirit, faith, and purity. Paul was saying that in reality Timothy's testimony would bring respect from those to whom he wanted to minister. Whether Timothy's youthfulness was actually hindering his effectiveness in ministry, we do not know. Evidently he thought it was.

What is interesting is that virtually everyone thinks that something about himself will cause others to despise him. For Timothy it was his youth. He apparently thought, *"No one will listen to me because I am young."* How many times I have heard an older person say, *"No one will listen to me because I am old."* Others can be heard saying, *"No one will listen to me because I am poor, not well educated, a new believer, low on the totem pole, not in the circle, etc."* Every reader of this book may have a reason of his own about why he feels his attempts to influence others for Christ will leave him despised. Paul told Timothy of the one thing he had available to him that could not be legitimately despised by anyone—the reality of his example.

What is amazing is that today the people who often feel most despised are parents. Parents feel like their children will listen to and believe just about everyone else, but them. Perhaps Paul would say, *"Let no child despise you as a parent, but be thou an example to your child in word, in conversation, in charity, in spirit, in faith, and in purity."* The simplest definitions of these terms are: word (how you talk), conversation (how you live), charity (your love for others), spirit (your attitudes), faith (your trust in the Lord), and purity (your single-heartedness for the things of God).

The godly parent's example can never be denied by a child. It is the strongest means of impact a dad or mom has available to influence a child for righteousness. To fail in this area is to fail a child in the worst possible way. Many voices vie for a child's ear and many influences try to reach his heart. The tempter will have no mercy as he tries to get a child to fall. The world is filled with opportunities for momentary sinful pleasures. The child himself is drawn away of his own lust, as the old nature pressures him from within. In the midst of it all, he needs something genuine and true to which he can turn. Something must be ever before him that says there is a better way that alone brings satisfaction to the soul and peace to the heart. The testimony to the value of serving the Lord and refusing sin must be the consistent life of a parent—a parent who demonstrates in every situation that God's way is the best way.

The truth of *what we are* should be a source of great motivation to any parent who longs for his children to love and serve the Lord. Our Lord could say to His disciples, *"Follow me"* (Matthew 9:9). Paul could say, *"Brethren, be followers together of me, and mark them which walk so as ye have us for an example"* (Philippians 3:17). Paul gave a powerful testimony to the believers of Thessalonica in his first letter to them. He said in chapter 1, verses 5-7, *"For our gospel came not unto you in word only, but also in power, and in the Holy Ghost, and in much assurance; as ye know what manner of men we were among you for your sake. And ye became followers of us, and of the Lord,…so that ye were examples to all that believe in Macedonia and Achaia."* The word *followers* means imitators, not in a fake or phony way, but in a genuine effort to be like their spiritual mentors. Parents should desire their children to follow them and give their children every good reason to follow. Would the believers at Thessalonica have followed the Lord if the lives of Paul and his companions had not been worthy of imitation? I think not! If parents live worthy of imitation, their children will follow, by God's grace. Unfortunately, Christians who have a good personal testimony sometimes rear children who have no heart for God.

One must remember that being an example is not the end of parenting, it is the beginning. Parenting involves training, controlling, teaching, loving, disciplining, protecting, and other elements—all of which must be administered according to scriptural admonition. There are also negative elements, such as, not provoking a child to wrath, nor bringing him to discouragement. Parenting takes an incredible amount of time, attention, and work.

A faithful example is foundational to successful parenting, but it must be supported by all the other aspects of parental obligation. In later chapters we will address the other factors in successful parenting. However, being an example is first and foremost as a parental duty. A deaf ear will be turned to a dad or mom who talk Christianity and go through the motions for the sake of others, but have little heart for God. It was the Savior who quoted Isaiah the prophet in Matthew 15:8, *"This people draweth nigh unto me with their mouth, and honoureth me with their lips; but their heart is far from me."* Though no one else may ever figure it out, our children will know if such words apply to us.

Please do not be afraid to take an honest look at yourself. Too much is at stake to continue down a path that may cost you your children. No perfect parents exist, but children do not expect perfection. Thankfully, most children are willing to forgive honest mistakes and normal human failures found in their parents. Hypocrisy, however, is hard for anyone to take when it is discovered in those who are in authority. Though we may be weak, let us make every effort to be true to the Lord, true to ourselves, and true to our children.

3 Training A Child

in the way he should go

One of the most significant texts on the rearing of children is Proverbs 22:6—*"Train up a child in the way he should go: and when he is old, he will not depart from it."* I do not know if any other verse in the Bible has been interpreted in so many different ways as this one.

One interpretation teaches that while children may grow up and go away from the Lord for a time, there is always hope that some day they will come back to serve Him. No doubt, parents with wayward children should both hope and pray for their children to return to the Lord, but that is not what this verse is all about.

Another interpretation suggests that a parent should discover the various tendencies in a child and make sure to encourage development in those areas. For instance, if a child likes music, make sure he takes music lessons; if he likes athletics, make sure he plays on a team. This may be the worst of the interpretations.

More recently I have heard some say that the verse is a mere principle with no promise attached to it. That interpretation declares that the concept of the verse is generally true, but one cannot really depend on it for hope in producing the right kind of child. This view doesn't give much hope to parents who are rearing children in this wicked day. It serves more to excuse the parent who has failed in rearing a child to grow up to serve Christ.

My counsel—take the verse for what it says. Begin to get extremely serious about training your children according to the teaching of the Bible.

Let's examine what it says. Notice the text begins with the word *train*. The term is not *raise*. If you have crops or animals, you are raising them. To raise an animal, just give it enough food and time and sure enough it will get big. Some people seem to think that is the extent of their obligation toward their children. Not so! Millions of young people have been raised without ever getting properly trained. Also note, the term is not *teach*. We need to teach our children and we will discuss that later, but our obligation to our children is more than teaching. It is not unusual to hear a parent rebuke a child by saying, *"You know better than that."* That statement suggests the child has been taught, but not necessarily trained *better than that*.

To *train* includes the concepts of molding character and establishing direction. This is our task in parenting. If parents do not mold godly character in their children and establish their lives with spiritual direction, they have not properly trained them. Children will surely end up with some kind of character and move through life in some direction. But will it be what we want for them as Christians or will they end up conformed to the world around them?

Let's go further. The root meaning of the word translated *train* is to compact or narrow down. We find this word elsewhere in the Bible translated by the words *dedicate* and *dedicated*. The term is used to describe Solomon's actions after he built the Temple of the Lord. In I Kings 8:63 we read, *"...So the king and all the children of Israel dedicated the house of the LORD."* When Solomon dedicated the Temple he was "narrowing down" the use of that building. The Temple was built for worshipping and glorifying God and would be used for no other purpose. That very same word is translated in Proverbs 22:6 as *train*. As parents we are to *narrow down* the experience of our children to "the way they should go."

The text says, *"...And when he is old, he will not depart from it."* This text is filled with hope for the parent who truly cares how his child will turn out. Unfortunately, many parents are ignoring or intentionally disobeying this very important verse from Scripture. The children of Christian homes are gaining extremely broad experiences with the things of this world; often, while they are quite young.

Think of the ways we allow our children to be introduced to the sinfulness and allurements of the world. TV and video tapes are stand out examples of how the world invades our homes. The average child spends from three to six hours per day in front of the TV. This time is often unsupervised in spite of the fact that programming designed for children presents hours of information, activities, and entertainment that are foreign to Christianity. While one would hope that video tapes rented and specifically brought into the home would offer far better material, it is often not the case. Instead of "narrowing" the experience of children, parents are often the very ones who allow the philosophies and practices of the world to be presented to their little ones.

Without a doubt, our children are going to learn about the world at some point, but their innocence must be maintained as long as possible. When they do see and experience the things of the world, we want them to see it all on Christian terms and we want them to see the world for what it really is. When a child learns about alcohol, for instance, he should hear about it as a life and home destroyer—perhaps through the testimony of someone who has been gloriously saved. He should not see it in a TV setting where people are partying and seemingly having a great time.

For now, let this thought sink into your mind. Through word, example, and experience we want to make sure our children are guided into *the way they should go*. That means parents must take responsibility for all that their children see, hear, and do. The training experience involves controlling, teaching, loving, and a variety of other related skills—all designed to help the child make godly, spiritual choices. The goal is to lead him toward a life that will honor the Lord. No other way can be acceptable to the Christian parent.

Controlling Our Children

A beginning element in the process of training our children is the challenge to control them. Few people need to be convinced that most children today are out of control. Go into the mall or shopping center and watch as parents come by with their children. Children are so disrespectful. I have been tempted to enter into a situation to aid a floundering mother. She wants to go one way, but her child has chosen another direction. Before long there may be crying, hitting, kicking, yelling, or even spitting—and sometimes the kids do it, too (only kidding). Can we help but wonder what those parent/child relationships will become over the ensuing years?

From time to time a parent will come in frustration to ask what can be done about their teenager, who is now totally out of control. As I have stated publicly dozens of times, I have always wanted to ask that parent, "When did that child get out of control?" God, in His grace, planned life so we receive our children when they are very small and ignorant of the prevailing wickedness of the world. When we bring them home from the hospital they have seen little, heard little, and done little. They are totally under our control. The parent's battle will be to keep them that way.

So when do they get out of control? Is it when they begin to crawl, or when they walk, or when they talk? When does it happen? This I know, by the age of 6 months (and probably earlier) those precious little ones begin to communicate that they want it their way. It may be screaming at meal time, kicking at changing time, or crying until they are picked up. But, whenever and however, it is not long before they begin to manifest their own will.

Obviously parents have to be sensitive and discerning, so they can be alert to the possibility of something truly being wrong. The attentive mom will soon learn, however, the difference between the cries of pain and discomfort versus the early expressions of anger and willfulness. From his earliest days it must be determined that this little one will not be allowed to get out of control. Listen dad and mom—in the conflict of wills with that precious child, you *must* win!

Effective control can begin by using the word—*NO*. Expressing it firmly and somewhat sharply will quickly let a young child know that his actions are unacceptable. It is a powerful tool. When at other times we talk sweetly and happily to convey approval, our children will rapidly learn the difference. The time will come when the *NO* will be well reinforced by an appropriate slap on the back of the hand. If, for instance, you tell your little one *NO* and he persists in grabbing a forbidden item, the slap on the hand will let him know you are serious. The slap does not have to be particularly hard. Just coupling it with the *NO* will strengthen the impact of your discipline.

Contributing to the effectiveness of these actions will be the use of your eyes. Begin early making your child look at you when you are talking to him. Let me emphasize that. MAKE YOUR CHILD LOOK AT YOU WHEN YOU ARE TALKING TO HIM. Call his name and say, *"Look at me."* If you have not done this, start today. Your attempts to get eye-to-eye contact may be a revelation to you of the willfulness of your child. He will not want to look at you, especially if he has done wrong. Eye contact is a powerful tool—to assure that a child understands what you are requesting—and, equally powerful, in bringing conviction in a time of discipline.

In the glorious description of the Lord Jesus in Revelation 1:14, John tells us that His eyes were as a flame of fire. Someday you and I will have to look into those eyes to give an account of ourselves at the Judgment Seat of Christ. It may be the most difficult experience we will ever have to face.

Some years ago I had the opportunity to visit some believers in Germany. On the Lord's Day I attended their services and participated at the Lord's Table. They shared a common cup (everyone drank from the same cup). When it was passed from one person to the next, it was required that their eyes had to meet. The purpose was to bring conviction in preparation for taking the cup. It was a very interesting and thought provoking experience.

Do not ignore the marvelous God-given tool of eye contact in dealing with your children. Require them to look at you when you give them instruction and when you express rebuke. You will be amazed at the difference it will make. By the way, make good use of your eyes in the whole process of training. Eyes can convey love, anger, disappointment, or joy. Let them work for you in reaching your child's heart and conscience.

Controlling your child is where training begins. If you are not successful in this critical area, you will struggle in the whole process. I know that some people have one particular child that is uniquely uncontrollable. You may be in that situation, too. Believe this, when the Lord gave instructions about rearing children, He knew your little one would come along someday. Yours may be tougher than some others, but you still must keep him under control.

One of the most sobering statements in the Bible is the condemnation of a household where the father did not control his children. The Lord spoke to Samuel about Eli in I Samuel 3:13-14. He said, *"For I have told him that I will judge his house for ever for the iniquity which he knoweth; because his sons made themselves vile, and he restrained them not. And therefore I have sworn unto the house of Eli, that the iniquity of Eli's house shall not be purged with sacrifice nor offering for ever."* None of us would want that judgment pronounced upon us or our family. CONTROL your children!

Little ones must not be allowed to do wrong, nor dare we let them refuse to do what is right. They must receive clear instructions and be required to follow them. If they succeed in ignoring or rejecting your authority, you will face a life of great sorrow. An old saying goes something like this: *"When children are little they walk on your feet, when they get older they walk on your heart."* Thankfully, it does not have to be that way.

(Discussion of the *rod of correction* and its biblical use is found in chapter 4).

Teaching Our Children

A second factor in training is the necessity to teach. When our children are young, control takes precedence. Children must or must not do some things when they are young, but they may not be able to understand the whys and wherefores of the standards of our home.

For instance, a four year old may come in to inform us that he has been invited to attend the movie theater with the child next door. At that point he only needs to know that permission is denied, because ours is a Christian home. He can return to thank the neighbor for the kind invitation, but must decline because dad and mom said, "No." When the same scenario occurs a few years later, it may be time to sit him down and teach him why we as Christians do not go to certain places nor do certain things.

For instance, have you ever thought through why Christians have traditionally avoided movie theaters? I Thessalonians 5:22 says *"Abstain from all appearance of evil."* Movie theaters typically offer a menu of stories filled with violence, alcohol, drugs, immorality, and a very unhealthy dose of the world's philosophy and values. When a Christian attends, he takes it all in personally and also weakens his testimony before others by giving the appearance of feeding on the ungodly content of the films. Of course, it is not the facility that is the problem. If someone can find a public theater that is known to show only good, wholesome, and perhaps Christian movies, one might go in good conscience. Usually the typical theater brings in a "good" movie from time to time, but we can avail ourselves of good movies from a number of sources and bring them into our home without harming our testimony. I do not have to go to the theater, which is known for the wrong kind of movies, to see the good one. I might be able to buy a soda in a bar, but bars are known for alcohol, so I get my soda somewhere else. I might see a good movie at the local theater, but theaters are known for Hollywood's worst offerings, so we get our good movies somewhere else.

Children cannot be expected to grow up and live their lives based on their parent's convictions. Eventually they will have to make choices. Parents want to be sure those choices are based on the Word of God. And in order for children to make those choices, they will have to be taught biblical principles that will take them through life in a God-honoring way. Early on, you will want to bring to your child's attention a verse like I Corinthians 10:31 that states, *"Whether therefore ye eat, or drink, or whatsoever ye do, do all to the glory of God."* A chapter and verse does not necessarily exist for every situation that will come your child's way; but through a single text, memorized, and put into practice, he can be delivered from falling into an incredible amount of temptation. The commitment to *"do all to the glory of God"* will keep him out of the movie theater and numerous other sinful situations for the rest of his life.

I Corinthians 6:12 offers similar protections when it states, *"All things are lawful unto me, but all things are not expedient: all things are lawful for me, but I will not be brought under the power of any."* In this day of addictions and horrendous peer pressure, a young person needs to determine that he *"will not be brought under the power of any."* The term *power* means domination and enslavement. It is wonderful that through the enablement of Jesus Christ we can successfully refuse enslavement to anyone or anything except our blessed Savior Himself. If we build this principle into the lives of our children, think of the glorious liberty they can enjoy from the sorrows of this world.

Teaching is not all there is to training, but it plays a large part in the process. Let's consider the instruction Moses gave in Deuteronomy 6 to get further help with this matter of directing our children in *the way they should go.*

Deuteronomy 6:6-7 states, *"And these words which I command thee this day, shall be in thine heart: And thou shalt teach them diligently unto thy children, and shalt talk of them when thou sittest in thine house, and when thou walkest by the way, and when thou liest down, and when thou risest up."*

Moses told parents to *"teach…diligently."* These two words are a single term in Hebrew which means to sharpen by repetition. The subject matter for teaching was to be the Word of God and the students were their own children. Are your children "sharp" in their knowledge of the Scriptures and Scriptural truth? Think of the character traits that you would like to see built into your child's life. Now realize that you have to do the building.

Godly qualities such as patience, loyalty, diligence, faithfulness, honesty, and trustworthiness are needed for a successful, Christ-honoring testimony. Conviction in these areas will not develop by chance. A plan must exist to make it happen. Moses gave important insight regarding this when he said, *"…And shalt talk of them when thou sittest in thine house, and when thou walkest by the way, and when thou liest down, and when thou riseth up."* These little phrases speak to us of the daily routine of life. Effective parenting occurs when Scripture is brought into daily experience.

A parent cannot teach his child diligence in a 15-minute devotional around the breakfast table. That devotional time is important, but diligence will be taught when a father and son are out working in the yard together and the son wants to stop, though the task is not quite done. Dad's encouragement to finish the job together sows the seeds of diligence.

Loyalty can be taught when a son is on a team, but does not play much, so he wants to quit. Requiring allegiance to the team at that point makes the difference.

Faithfulness can be taught when a daughter had promised to clean her room, but now has an invitation to go away for the day with a friend. While on occasion a parent might yield in a given situation, the character quality of swearing to ones own hurt (Psalm 15:4) can be strengthened at such a time.

Repetitious guidance and being available for those day-to-day teaching opportunities takes time and sacrifice. As a matter of fact, good parenting takes much more time than most parents are willing to invest in their children. Somewhere along the way we swallowed the line that it is not the quantity of time, but the quality of time that matters. Parenting requires both!

Let's be honest. We are busy people, but we can generally make time for what we really want to do. A lady may be busy, but an invitation to go shopping with a friend can somehow get worked into the schedule. A man can be overwhelmed with paperwork, but he can somehow get away from the office early enough to get in nine holes of golf before going home for the evening.

The truth is—time with their children is not high on the priority list of many parents. It needs to be high on your list. Other things will wait, but children grow rapidly. Years fly by, never to be recovered once they are lost. No parent will ever regret sacrificing other things to spend time with their children. But thousands now regret letting other things crowd their children out of their lives.

Let me add this to the challenge. It is not just time with all the kids that is necessary—it is time with each one individually. Remember that each one of your children is different. One is athletic, one is not. One is academically sharp, one is not. One loves to play an instrument, one hates it. The point is that each one needs individual attention. Consider a family that has five children. Four could grow up to love and serve the Lord, but one could choose the path of worldliness and sin. It is amazing that he could be raised in the same home, have the same parents, attend the same church, and yet goes an entirely different direction from his siblings. Never forget, he is an individual child with individual needs. Each child needs one-on-one love, attention, understanding, and discipline.

It is fair to hope that good teaching will come from other sources in support of what we as parents are trying to do. Maybe a good Sunday School teacher, athletic coach, or grandparent will aid the cause of training our children—but parents must accept the responsibility. Determine to think of it this way: If you don't teach your child honesty (for example), no one will. Now how are you going to accomplish that goal? Face the same challenge with each child and with every character quality he needs to learn. Does the task seem overwhelming? It should, but that is parenting.

The message Moses was trying to convey is that our children will face all kinds of experiences as they go through life (sitting in the house, walking by the way, lying down, and rising up). That's when someone must be there to show them how to live. That someone must be a godly parent.

In Deuteronomy 6:8-9, Moses introduced another area of teaching. He said, *"And thou shalt bind them for a sign upon thine hand, and they shall be as frontlets between thine eyes. And thou shalt write them upon the posts of thy house, and on thy gates."*

In verse 8, he was introducing the Jewish phylacteries, small leather bands wrapped around the forehead and the hand. Inserted into each were small portions of Scripture. We do not advocate this uniquely Jewish practice for the New Testament Christian. In verse 9, he called for Scripture to be printed on the posts and gates of the house. The underlying principle in these verses is significant and can be applied to us today. Moses instructed the parents of Israel to continually present visual reminders of God and His Word to their families. Perhaps even more foundational was the challenge to guard their children's eyes.

Today's Christian homes should be filled with the message of God. Plaques, pictures, posters, and other items should present Scripture verses and spiritual truths in every house. Young people should be reminded as they move from room to room that *Christ is the head of this house; As for me and my house, we will serve the Lord; I can do all things through Christ which strengtheneth me;* etc. Worldly posters, as found in the rooms of many teens, only undermine what the Christian home represents.

Also, as was addressed in the first chapter of this book, we must protect our children from TV programs and videos, as well as other material that may corrupt their minds and hearts. The eye gate is one of the most important avenues for taking in information. It must be guarded.

How many Christian adults live with haunting memories of things they once saw, but now they wish they could forget. David fell because he *saw* Bathsheba (II Samuel 11:2). He later wrote in Psalm 101:3, *"I will set no wicked thing before mine eyes."* How much heartache and sin would have been avoided if he had made that commitment early in life. In I John 2:16 we are warned about the lust of the eyes. Proverbs 27:20 says, *"Hell and destruction are never full; so the eyes of man are never satisfied."* Moses wanted to be sure that the youth of Israel saw the right things. We must do the same for our children.

Teaching is very important to successful training. Under this heading we must include not only what we want children to learn, but also what we do not want them to learn. If you are a parent, you are the primary teacher of your children. As important as it is that we control our children, to do so without teaching them the principles on which the Christian life is built is to ask for rebellion as they reach an age when they want to know WHY.

Loving Our Children

It would be rare indeed if parents had to be instructed or challenged to love their children. It is not unusual, however, for parents to need encouragement and help in expressing that love. I have heard comments like "My father never told me he loved me." That statement might often be followed up with "Oh, I am sure he did, but he never said it to me." Another equally common statement is "I don't know how to show love to my children, because my parents never really showed love to me." One more I have heard from time to time is "Back then parents just did not say I love you nor do a lot of hugging." It is important that your children never have to make any such statements.

I am grateful the Lord did not hesitate to demonstrate His love for us. *"But God commendeth his love toward us, in that, while we were yet sinners, Christ died for us"* (Romans 5:8). The Lord loves us and we never have to wonder about it. Parental expression of love is the catalyst in successful child rearing. Love alone is not enough. Without the other elements of training it may create a very permissive home life, which would give children far too much liberty in choosing their own way. In turn, children would create many problems and heartaches for themselves. Control is necessary.

Control without love, however, produces far worse results. Excessive control without love brings anger, hatred, and bitterness—often extending beyond the authoritarian parent, reaching all the way to the Lord Himself. Proper discipline, undergirded by good teaching, can bring parental success when the home is dominated by a loving atmosphere.

It is somewhat common for outsiders (especially those who do not know the Lord) to think the Christian home is too disciplined. They believe the children are being deprived if they do not get a full taste of this world's wickedness. Christian parents are often warned that their strictness will produce rebellion. True enough, strictness can produce rebellion if it is not balanced with love and a genuine Christian testimony on the part of dad and mom.

Do you love your children? I am sure you do. Let them know it in a hundred different ways and let them know it everyday. *I love you!* What great words! As the kids go off to school, remind them. *I love you!* When they come home, when they go out to play, when they are going away, when they are going to bed, when a problem needs to be faced, when the need arises for discipline, when they finish the chores—*I love you!* Hug them, squeeze them (gently), rub their back—just to let them know *I love you!* Read to them, pray with them, play with them, take them special places, do special things, buy some treats, compliment their efforts—just to let them know *I love you!* Take time for them, answer their questions, teach them to ride a bike or roller skate, ask them about their day and listen attentively—just to let them know *I love you!* Laugh with them and cry with them—what great ways to say *I love you!* Get creative and add to this list dozens of other possibilities to convey it in your own way. *I love you!*

In training our children, the tough times will come. Expressions of rebellion will show up, stubbornness will be evidenced, and deceitfulness will be discovered. God said that foolishness is bound in the heart of a child. Never forget—it is in every child, though it may be manifested in different ways. When the foolishness shows up in one form of confrontation or another, the parents must win the conflict. When the crisis of the moment is over, however, the child must rest in total assurance that he is loved. He may have been rebuked, restricted, or paddled and he may have hurt feelings or lingering anger, but he must know deep in his heart that he is loved. He may even offer the argument that you do not love him; but your challenge is to so overwhelm him with expressions of love that deep in his heart he will know he is the object of your deepest affection. Some children are easier to "love" than others. A parent must work hard to counteract the tendency of some children to misinterpret the disapproval of their actions as conveying a lack of love.

Never forget that love involves sacrifice. Many times children are ignored and left to themselves, because of the many demands placed on adults today through work, church activities, and other interests. Church should hold a place of priority for the family and the marriage relationship itself must be strengthened by time alone for dad and mom. At the same time, we must make sacrifices for our children. Little things like parental attendance at a piano recital or a ball game can mean so much to a child.

When I played Little League Baseball my mother worked to keep us kids; but she would rush from work to the field, even if she only could be there for the last inning. It meant more to me than words could tell. During a few years of coaching high school basketball, I watched young people look for their parents in the stands. For some of those boys, no parent ever arrived. It broke their hearts. Other things can always take our time if we let them. Parents must remember that children are at home for only a few years. To sacrifice some of our wants to meet some of their needs will be an investment that will pay rich rewards in the days ahead.

Some Final Thoughts

Is it possible to do it right? Can we really see our children grow up to love the Lord and reject the world? Not only is it possible—we must refuse any other option. In fact, we should dare to reach for higher ground in the rearing of our children. Let's not settle for spiritual mediocrity. Let's not be content with the assurance that our children are saved. The cause of Christ needs more than born-again spectators in the battle for truth.

Consider these words of God spoken about Abraham in Genesis 18:19—*"For I know him, that he will command his children and his household after him, and they shall keep the way of the LORD, to do justice and judgment; that the LORD may bring upon Abraham that which he hath spoken of him."* These words are quite different than what the Lord said about Eli and his house, aren't they? Notice that both statements are founded upon the actions of the parents. Eli did not restrain his sons, while Abraham commanded his children after him.

This statement regarding Abraham was more fully discussed in the first chapter, but consider one part of this telling verse again—*"They shall keep the way of the LORD."* The term *keep* means to guard or preserve and the term *way* means a trodden path. That expression describes the children we want. If we raise up a group of mere churchgoers, they are not going to have much impact for God (and who knows what our grandchildren will be). We want children who will stand up in a wicked society, ready to guard and preserve the trodden path of God. When that occurs we can rejoice in success as parents.

Do not allow yourself to be discouraged by what you see in families around you. Most parents are not seriously pursuing biblical parenting. Parents want their children to turn out right, but wanting good things is not enough. A price will be paid to see our children grow up to love and honor the Savior. The price includes much time and effort, coupled with careful devotion to the Bible's teachings on child training. Take heart! The Lord gave you children that they might bring glory to Him. He has told you what to do and how to do it. You will not be a perfect parent and you will not rear perfect children; however, by God's grace and through his Word, you can see your children grow up to love you and to love the Lord you serve.

4 PADDLING WITH A PURPOSE

This chapter needs careful consideration, because we live in a violent society. In reaction to increasing violence, many reject the biblical teaching on paddling, interpreting loving discipline as a form of violence. Sometimes that view is fostered by Christian parents who, along with the world, are ignorant of the nature and practice of godly parenting. The use of the rod and the concept of paddling, as taught in Scripture, is essential to rearing our children properly. The appropriate use of the rod will not be violent and it will not teach violence.

Sometimes the use of the rod is rejected for other reasons. I have heard parents say, "We just gave up paddling our boy, because no matter how often we disciplined him that way, it did not work." Still others have said, "We don't paddle our little girl. All you have to do is look at her when she has done something wrong and she bursts into tears. So, why paddle her?"

Did you know, God never told parents to judge whether or not paddling works, nor did he say that the goal of paddling was to bring tears? The purpose of paddling is to drive foolishness out of the heart. We dare not reject what God has said based on our experience or understanding. He knows what is right, because He made us. As we consider what the Bible says on this critical topic, determine to follow the Word of God carefully and "paddle with a purpose"—God's purpose!

Let's begin by breaking down the primary biblical text on paddling. Proverbs 22:15 states, *"Foolishness is bound in the heart of a child; but the rod of correction shall drive it far from him."* Immediately we are introduced to the purpose of paddling and we must never lose sight of it. The purpose of paddling is to drive foolishness out of a child's heart and, therefore, successfully keep him from becoming a fool. The text does not say the child is a fool. He is not! Foolishness, however, is bound in his heart and if it is not driven out, he will become a fool.

Notice the word *bound*. An understanding of this term will help us grasp the importance of proper discipline. While it is translated bound here, in most places the same word is translated conspire or conspiring. Think this through. Foolishness is not bound, as if chained, in the child's heart; but instead it is conspiring in the child's heart. To conspire speaks of plotting, planning, and undermining. The Bible teaches us that foolishness is constantly working its destructive ways in a child's heart. To appreciate the seriousness of this condition, we need to understand what the heart is.

A cursory study of the Scriptures reveals that the heart is the deepest part of our being. The term is sometimes used interchangeably with the word *spirit* when referring to the human spirit. This parallel usage is found in Psalm 51:17 where David said, *"The sacrifices of God are a broken spirit: a broken and a contrite heart, O God, thou wilt not despise."* Isaiah quoted God in Isaiah 57:15 when he wrote, *"...I dwell in the high and holy place, with him also that is of a contrite and humble spirit, to revive the spirit of the humble, and to revive the heart of the contrite ones."* Without question, what goes on in the heart/spirit of a person is critical to his spiritual well being.

Consider what the Bible says about the workings of the heart. For instance, the heart is the place where sin is acknowledged, purposes are established, and values are formed. In Romans 10:9-10 Paul wrote, *"That if thou shalt confess with thy mouth the Lord Jesus, and shalt believe in thine HEART that God hath raised him from the dead, thou shalt be saved. For with the HEART man believeth unto righteousness; and with the mouth confession is made unto salvation."* Might foolishness working in a child's heart hinder him from trusting Christ as Savior? In Proverbs 23:7 we read, *"For as he thinketh in his HEART, so is he:..."* Proverbs 4:23 says, *"Keep thy HEART with all diligence; for out of it are the issues of life."* Outward obedience may veil inward rebellion for a while, but in due time the heart will manifest itself in outward actions.

The heart must be tender before the Lord and diligently guarded from corrupting influences. In Daniel 1:8 we read, *"Daniel purposed in his HEART that he would not defile himself..."* If Daniel was not committed to the Lord in the depths of his being, he would have found it easy to surrender under the incredible pressure of his situation. His pure heart gave him the conviction to stand for what was right, when circumstances might have seemingly justified compromise. No one can afford to have foolishness tampering with his heart.

Other texts would inform us that pride, deception, and bitterness are sins of the heart. The Lord Jesus said in Matthew 15:19, *"For out of the HEART proceed evil thoughts, murders, adulteries, fornications, thefts, false witness, blasphemies."* Proverbs 14:10 states, *"The HEART knoweth his own bitterness."* Jeremiah 17:9 reads, *"The HEART is deceitful above all things, and desperately wicked: who can know it?"*

On the other hand, spiritual wisdom, discernment, uprightness, revival, and true surrender to the Lord are all experiences of the heart. Think how important it is that the heart be right before God. So much is at stake.

Perhaps the most sobering text of all regarding the heart is Psalm 14:1 that says, *"The fool hath said in his HEART, there is no God."* A person's rejection of God is not a matter of intellectual consideration; it is a matter of the heart, not the head. God tells us in His Word that man has every reason to believe in God's existence and power. In the face of overwhelming evidence many still deny him. Why? Because they are fools. To deny God, one would have to be a fool; but how does he become a fool? He begins life with foolishness conspiring in his heart as a child and foolishness successfully brings him to complete ruination. Foolishness fully developed will take one toward the depths of sin's potential.

Every parent must face the seriousness of what is going on in his/her child's heart. Could any parental challenge be more serious? We can thank the Lord that our text offers hope regarding the work of foolishness in the heart, when it states, *"...but the rod of correction shall drive it far from him."* Here the Lord gives the remedy for foolishness. Let's examine this second part of the verse.

The word rendered *correction* is translated 30 times in the Bible as the word *instruction*. Please take note that the rod is not a "rod of punishment." Punishment focuses on the offence that has been committed and is carried out with a view toward making the offender suffer for his wrong. Instruction and correction look to the future, so the child will learn for days, and hopefully years to come. Every time the rod is used, it should be with the hope and intent that the foolishness in the child's heart will be diminished and that gradual improvement will occur in the child's behavior.

Let's talk about the "rod" itself. We need to understand what it is, and what it is not. The word *rod* in the phrase "rod of correction" is not the same as the term *rod* in the phrase "rod of Aaron." The "rod" of Aaron was the Hebrew *mattaw*, a branch. The "rod" of correction is the Hebrew *sheybet*, a small round stick. The term *sheybet* is found in II Samuel 18:14. The situation described in the verse is not a very nice one, but it serves to help us understand the meaning of the word—*"Then said Joab, I may not tarry thus with thee. And he took three darts in his hand, and thrust them through the heart of Absalom, while he was yet alive in the midst of the oak."* The term *darts* is the same word as the term *rod* from our text. Now a man's heart is about as big as his fist, so if Joab put three darts through Absalom's heart, the darts were rather small. The "rod" of correction is not very large.

Consider Judges 5:14 where we read, *"...and out of Zebulun they that handle the pen of the writer."* Here the term *pen* is the same term that is translated "rod" in our text. It is obvious that we are not talking about a very big stick when we talk about the "rod" of correction. This is why the writer of Proverbs 23:13-14 said, *"Withhold not correction from the child: for if thou beatest him with the rod, he shall not die. Thou shalt beat him with the rod, and shalt deliver his soul from hell."* The writer was telling parents they do not need to be afraid to use the "rod" when disciplining. You see, you can't beat a child to death with a dart or a pen.

What's the point? The rod is not an instrument that was ever intended to break a bone or produce any kind of serious injury. Discipline with the "rod" is not violent, nor will it produce violence. Perhaps the best way to understand what is intended as a rod is to think of the "switch," that slender flexible stick that can be broken off a shrub. It will sting, but never bring injury or damage to the child we love. Amazingly, God says the rod of correction will drive foolishness from the heart of our child. We may not understand how or why this is accomplished, but God affirms it. Only as we believe and practice the Scriptures can we have hope for our children. No other verse in the Bible is as clear as Proverbs 22:15 in demonstrating the purpose and power of the rod. Do you believe God knows what he is talking about? If so, remember he said, *"foolishness is bound in the heart of a child."* God is talking about every child.

Sometimes parents get deceived when it comes to the use of the rod. Remember we mentioned the parents who gave up the rod and tried other things? Whether or not using the rod seems to work or seems to be necessary, we need to follow God's instructions. God knows more about our children than we do and He made two very clear statements. First, foolishness is bound in the heart of a child (every child) and second, the rod of correction is what drives it far from him. Even that precious little girl who cries when you look at her needs the rod; and that terror of a boy needs it, too—even when it seems to do no good. Why? God said so!

The use of the rod is being set aside by many Christian parents. They use time outs, take away privileges, send kids to their rooms, or just plain yell—but they refuse God's instruction. Commit yourself to obeying God's way. Our ultimate goal is to see wisdom prevail in the lives of our children.

Wisdom comes in a variety ways. *"The fear of the Lord is the beginning of wisdom." "The rod and reproof give wisdom."* Wisdom comes through the Scriptures. It can be gained through godly counsel and instruction and, in fact, can be learned by just observing others who live wisely. The development of wisdom, however, will be thwarted by the presence of foolishness. The use of the rod of correction is the God-ordained way to drive out the foolishness. Following Scripture will put you far ahead of those parents who think they can improve on God's way.

Another matter is brought to our attention regarding the use of the rod in Proverbs 13:24 and 19:18. The first text states, *"He that spareth his rod hateth his son: but he that loveth him chasteneth him betimes."* The term *betimes* literally means with the dawn. It does not mean we use the rod every morning (thankfully for children), but it speaks of being on top of a situation and recognizing its importance. For instance, if you have a project that must be done on a given day, you do not sleep in until noon. You might very well get up "with the dawn" to give the project the time and attention it deserves. So with our children—we must be diligent in our discipline, which will be one of our greatest testimonies of love.

The verse states that if the parent spares the rod he hates his son. Some would question that statement, claiming just the opposite. Many parents have said they did not paddle their children because they loved them. Why does the Bible say that to spare the rod means we hate our children? If we really believe that (as God says) the proper use of the rod is what will keep a child from becoming a fool, then to refuse the rod must mean we hate him. One of the worst things a parent could do to a child is to let his foolishness go unchallenged, allowing him to become a fool as described in the Scriptures. If the parent loves the child, he will use the rod in accordance with biblical teaching.

The challenge of Proverbs 19:18 is similar—*"Chasten thy son while there is hope, and let not thy soul spare for his crying."* The warning—to not let the parent's soul spare for the child's crying—assures us that godly parents find no joy in disciplining their children. To have to discipline is not an easy obligation to fulfill, but it must be done in the interest of every child.

A sense of urgency is built into this text. The parent is to chasten *while there is hope.* The phrase *while there is hope* is significant. The word *hope* literally means cord and speaks of attachment. Of course, the physical cord of attachment to the child's mother is cut at birth; but dependency on and attachment to the parents is still an emotional and physical reality. The message of our text is that as the child gets older the attachment is gradually broken, as independence is developed. During the time of close attachment there is the greatest "hope" of having strong impact on the child. If we fail to accomplish important training goals while children are young, the time will come when hope may be lost.

Both these verses let us know that early child training is important. The foolishness working in the child's heart must not be allowed to develop. If we don't get busy about the business of training, our child can evidently get beyond hope. On the other hand, if we train him early, the kinds of physical confrontation between older children and parents heard of in some homes will never be faced in ours. By the time a child is eleven or twelve years old he should have developed deep affection and respect for his parents that has been produced through loving and consistent discipline. This will happen when he is chastened early. One thing we can guarantee—the better job parents do when the children are young, the easier it will be when the children get older.

We learn from other texts that the use of the rod is to be coupled with appropriate reproof. As was intimated above, the time should come when the rod will no longer be needed and will be totally replaced by expressions of reproof. Proverbs 29:15 reads, *"The rod and reproof give wisdom: but a child left to himself bringeth his mother to shame."* The child left to himself is the undisciplined child and plenty of them bring shame and disappointment to their mothers. Notice in this text that reproof is coupled with the use of the rod. *To reprove* means to bring someone to what is right and not simply stop the wrong. Too often the disciplinary setting only ends the problem of the moment, but does not require the performance of what is right.

For instance, a child may be throwing his toys all around the room. It would not be unusual for a mother to stop her child, perhaps paddle him, and then pick up all the toys in a fit of frustration. Have you ever heard a mom complaining about having to pick up after her children? Proper reproof stops the throwing of the toys, allows for paddling if necessary, and requires the child to do what is right. He picks up the toys and puts them where they belong.

An unwise parent is one who confesses it has not been worth the aggravation to conquer the stubborn child's will by requiring him to clean up after himself. Sometimes it is easier to pick up the toys, remake the bed, or hang up the clothes than to confront the rebellious, forgetful, or lazy child requiring him to perform the duty he shirked. This kind of parenting, however, opens the door to more foolishness.

The combination of the rod and reproof gives wisdom. The properly disciplined child soon learns to stop his foolishness, because he will gain the knowledge that disobedience can result in getting the rod of correction and still having the task of cleaning up his own mess. Parental consistency will eventually show a child the value of doing an assigned task and doing it right the first time.

Proverbs 29:17 offers this hope—*"Correct thy son, and he shall give thee rest; yea he shall give delight unto thy soul."* Tragically some parents are happiest when they are away from their own children. They dread summertime, when school is over, because the kids will be home every day. They love camp and VBS, when their kids will be gone. Vacations are more trouble than they are worth. To put it simply, they can't stand their own children. If that is true, parents should understand that the problem is their own fault. God planned children to be a delight to their parents—but if His teaching for family life is ignored, and if proper correction is not given, then children can bring much trouble and heartache. And, foolishness unchecked in a child's heart will produce a fool in adulthood. Our aim is to keep our child from becoming a fool. Instead we want to see him develop in wisdom.

As we succeed, we will learn the significance of Proverbs 17:10—*"A reproof entereth more into a wise man than an hundred stripes into a fool."* What a blessing when your child reaches that stage of maturity when all you have to do is speak, and he listens and obeys! The verse suggests, however, that if he grows up to become a fool, nothing will turn him around. Proverbs 13:1 states, *"A wise son heareth his father's instruction: but a scorner heareth not rebuke"* and Proverbs 15:5 reads, *"A fool despiseth his father's instruction: but he that regardeth reproof is prudent."* Your child was not born a fool, but he can become one. He was not born wise, but he can learn wisdom. The Bible makes it clear that our parenting practices will make the difference.

The Fool as Described in the Bible

The fool, as described in the Bible, is one who lives focused on himself, filled with pride, and intentionally ignorant of God. In the Scriptures three different terms are translated *fool*. They have different shades of meaning, but taken together convey the idea of stupidity (sometimes expressed in silliness and sometimes expressed in wickedness). One thing is sure—you don't want to be the parent of a fool.

Have you seen a full-grown fool lately or perhaps a teenager heading in that direction? Consider the characteristics ascribed to a fool in the Scriptures:

- Proverbs 1:7 tells us he despises wisdom and instruction.

- Proverbs 10:8 tells us he rejects authority.

- Proverbs 12:15 tells us he refuses counsel.

- Proverbs 12:16 tells us he has no self control.

- Proverbs 14:3 tells us he is proud.

- Proverbs 14:8 tells us he is deceitful.

- Proverbs 14:9 tells us he does not take sin seriously.

- Proverbs 17:10 tells us he refuses correction.

- Proverbs 17:24 tells us he is short-sighted.

- Proverbs 18:13 tells us he reacts without full knowledge of a situation.

- Proverbs 29:11 tells us he does not know when to be quiet.

Is it any wonder that the Bible informs us that the child left to himself *"bringeth his mother to shame"* (Proverbs 29:15) and that *"A foolish son is the calamity of his father:"* (Proverbs 19:13).

The Scriptures teach us the purpose associated with paddling—it is the parent's hope for delivering one's child from foolishness. For that purpose to be fulfilled, the rod must be used in a right way. Perhaps one of the best ways to address the manner of paddling is to elicit warnings from some of the Scriptures we have just listed. We want to be sure that parents are not playing the part of the fool themselves while trying to deliver their children from foolishness.

One error constantly made in parenting is carrying out discipline in anger. We just noted in Proverbs 12:16 that the fool has no self control. A parent cannot be successful, if he is unable to control himself, while supposedly correcting the words and actions of his child. The display of temper may intimidate the child, but intimidation should not be a parental goal. If a child is scared into confession of his wrong, he has only learned that he must submit because his parent is bigger and stronger. Parental rule, however, is not dependent on physical strength—it is primarily spiritual authority. A child must learn that parents are in charge, because the Lord appointed them to the task, not because of their size. Calm demeanor and quiet talking will be avenues of directing the child to the Lord in the disciplinary process. If discipline does not nudge the child toward the Lord, it will accomplish little.

Another error often made by parents is reacting to the surface situation, rather than taking the necessary time to find out all the facts. Proverbs 18:13 says that if one answers a matter before he hears it, it is folly and shame to him. Details of a situation may modify its seeming seriousness. It may be that an apparent wrong was just a mistake, poor judgment, or a reflection of immaturity, and not the rebellion or sin that it first appeared. While some action of discipline may be necessary, it should be appropriate to the true circumstances. Many parents have forfeited the respect of their children, because discipline was overly harsh and without real regard for truth. Wisdom is the ability to see a matter in its truest light, so the very best decision can be made in addressing it. How do we ultimately teach our children to be wise if we fail to demonstrate wisdom in our parenting?

Parents are sometimes shortsighted in dealing with their children. According to Proverbs 17:24, shortsightedness is another characteristic of the fool. In every situation the parent must be looking toward the child's future. The ultimate goal is to see the child grow up to know, love, and serve the Lord as a wise Christian adult. Unjust discipline can produce bitterness and anger in children that may defeat them spiritually for many years.

The Bible mentions in Proverbs 17:6b that the glory of children are their fathers. What a precious truth! God has built into children a great respect for their dad. They tend to put him on a pedestal. Unfortunately, dads keep falling off through inconsistency, unfairness, favoritism, selfishness, and other traits that undermine the child rearing process. Sometimes a parent disciplines more harshly because he is in a bad mood or is over tired. He expects his child to somehow take all that into consideration and overlook his parental shortcomings, but the same type of consideration is not afforded the child.

Parents are shocked when a teen (who had previously never been a problem) breaks out in open rebellion. The reason may be because the teen has been bottling up his anger and frustration until the time he thinks he can finally get away with expressing it. Discipline is not successful because it resolves the problem of the moment. Discipline is only successful if it produces long term spiritual results.

Practical Concerns in Using the Rod

Without question the Lord teaches the parent to use the rod, but it is important to use it in a God-honoring way. The guidelines that follow cannot be supported by biblical chapter and verse, but are suggested as appropriate to the spirit of Scriptural teaching.

A powerful testimony reflecting God's tenderness is recorded in Psalm 103:13-14—*"Like as a father pitieth his children, so the LORD pitieth them that fear him. For he knoweth our frame; he remembereth that we are dust."* Given as a help for us to know God, through watching a father, the text teaches us how to be a right kind of parent. The word *pitieth* speaks of compassion and understanding. The Lord remembers that we are but dust and, therefore, treats us compassionately. As dads and moms, we are to treat our children with tender compassion and understanding, even when we must discipline them. Consider the following:

1. Make sure the child understands parental instructions and expectations.

Sometimes parents assume a child should know better than to do certain things. Parents owe it to their child to make expectations well known and would do well to clarify instructions in given situations. If a child is to perform a certain task, parents should require the child to look at the them when instructions are given and then be required to repeat the instructions back to the parents, so everyone is sure of what is or is not to be done. A child will often claim discipline is unfair because he did not know what was expected. Let there be no doubt.

2. Be mindful of a child's level of maturity.

A child's level of maturity will, to some degree, determine his ability to respond to parental instruction. For instance, if a twelve year old is told to "never" do something again, he should understand the significance of "never." If a two year old is given the same instruction, he will not be mature enough to understand that "never" means "never." Requirements and corresponding discipline must be appropriate to the child's ability to understand, retain, and respond.

3. Paddle only when clear instructions have been violated.

Discipline will be most successful when children cannot deny they deserve it.

4. Paddle privately.

Too often parents discipline publicly to embarrass and humiliate their children. Sometimes publicly addressing problems is a parent's way to demonstrate to others that they do not tolerate their children's disobedience. These goals are totally inappropriate. Parents must not care what others think, nor should they get any satisfaction from embarrassing their children before others. Discipline should be private to accomplish the most. The goal is humiliation before the Lord, not people. Discipline should strengthen the ties between parent and child. Embarrassment will only create negative feelings in the child which may eventually become deep bitterness.

5. Be under control.

If a parent is upset and angry, he may want to send the child to a private place for a period of time before discipline is carried out. A few minutes alone will allow the parent to get himself in a right spirit to handle the problem and will give the child time to reflect on his wrong doing. For a parent to yell, bang, slam doors, or display temper in other ways is worthless and may close the door to effective correction.

6. Appeal to the child's conscience.

The conscience was given by the Lord to protect us from sin. It was designed to make us feel guilty. Often those in the field of worldly psychology attack the use of guilt, believing it will produce some kind of emotional harm. Actually, guilt is a wonderful gift from God to keep us on the path of righteousness. A wise person will welcome guilt; desiring, in fact, to feel guilty when he is out of harmony with God's will and Word. When a child does wrong, a parent must appeal to the conscience, so the child will feel guilt and acknowledge his wrong. If a child is asked WHY he did wrong, he will always have a good excuse to justify himself. "Why" appeals to a child's emotions. If a child is asked WHAT he did wrong, making him take responsibility for his words and actions, he will have to face his wrong doing and admit that he is guilty. "What" appeals to the conscience. When he acknowledges his guilt, he must also acknowledge he is worthy of discipline.

7. Point the child to the Lord.

For discipline to be effective it must ultimately be a spiritual experience. The young child must be taught that his disobedience is what the Lord calls sin. As the child recognizes sin in his life, he can come to appreciate early in life that the Lord Jesus suffered for his sin. When he does wrong, he should be shown that his sin is first an offence to the Lord, then an offence to others. If paddling is appropriate for the wrong doing, the child should be shown in Scripture that the Lord established paddling as the way parents should discipline. The goal is to help the child see that he has been entrusted to the parent by the Lord, but ultimately he is answerable to the Lord, not mom and dad.

8. Paddle firmly, but not abusively.

The Bible does not tell parents exactly how many times to swat the child with the rod. Remembering that the goal is spiritual submission, not physical submission, will help the parent do right. Calm and deliberate discussion about the wrong doing is the best way to help the child face his guilt. Requiring the child to maintain eye contact helps create a tender response to rebuke. Genuine spiritual concern over the problem, rather than great personal offence, aids in producing brokenness over sin. Successfully dealing with a child in these areas has convinced this writer that three swats with the rod is sufficient to reinforce words of reproof in the difficult moments of correction. The hope is that the child will manifest true repentance for his wrong—but if the desired results are not achieved, the parent must not resort to further paddling to break the will. His will is not located on his bottom. Consistency and steadiness in enforcing the standards of the home, coupled with a great deal of love, will bring the long term results the godly parent desires. The parent must not yield to feelings of frustration with one child who seems to be much more stubborn than his siblings. Standards must be maintained firmly, so the most difficult of children will realize they will always lose the battle when they rebel. They must be brought to the understanding that dad and mom always win.

9. Reaffirm love for the child.

A parent's love should never be called into question through a disciplinary experience. Words and actions during the time of correction are very important, but another important step in discipline is to reaffirm love for the child after paddling. Tender words such as, "I love you" and a gentle comforting hug will go a long way to convince the child that (while his actions were disapproved) he is very much loved. The child's response to expressions of love may be a good indicator of how successfully the discipline was carried out. A hug returned is a good sign. It is appropriate to pray with the child, too—to remind him that all of life is spiritual and that parental concerns are primarily that the child be right with the Lord. At times discipline will not yield the desired results. How wonderful it would be if every time a confrontation happened between a parent and a child, the child would end up crying repentantly and offering a genuine apology for doing wrong. Since that will not always happen, let parents be reminded that the discipline meted out on a given day is one small part of an overall training process. I have often encouraged people that you cannot always judge someone's parenting by what their child is at five, but rather see what he is at 25. Parents who are consistent and faithful to the Word of God will, by God's grace, see their children grow up to be godly adults. Along the way there will be times of testing.

10. Give the child a fresh start.

When the discipline is over, the parent should clarify previously given instructions and expectations, so the child will have the best chance of avoiding more trouble. He should then be sent out—being given a fresh start—with the problem at hand being put behind him. Requiring apologies to those he hurt or offended is not always the best thing to do. It is of little value to require an apology, if the child does not have genuine sorrow for the offence. The child can be instructed that he should be sorry and that an apology is appropriate; but all of us have seen a child forced to say "I'm sorry" without true repentance. It doesn't mean much to the offender or the one offended. Being able to give a fresh start so quickly reveals one of the advantages of paddling over other means of discipline. Grounding or taking away privileges makes the unhappiness of discipline last for an hour, a day, a week, or however long the discipline lasts. Paddling God's way allows the problem to be resolved speedily with things getting back to normal in a short span of time.

While this chapter does not exhaust the subject of discipline with the rod, it gives basic guidelines to help Christian parents succeed in attaining spiritual impact on their children, when carrying out the difficult task of paddling. The reader is encouraged to review this chapter and think carefully through every disciplinary situation.

5 DISCIPLINE

Doing it right

In this chapter, we want to consider a number of guidelines to keep us on track in our whole disciplinary procedure. Parents will want to do some things all the time, and other things they must never do. If we can get the good things firmly settled in our minds, it will help us avoid serious mistakes in discipline, especially during those times when we might be wrestling with anger or frustration. An ounce of prevention being worth a pound of cure is never more true than in child rearing. Consider the following:

Never Slap or Punch Your Child

Parental authority is spiritual authority. If that point gets to the hearts of parents, it can make a tremendous difference in parenting. Parents are not in charge because they are bigger or stronger than their children; they are in charge because God says so. The Lord entrusts children to parents to be reared for His glory.

When a parent slaps or punches, it is a clear demonstration of ignorance regarding parental obligation and privilege. I have seen fathers slap their boys on the back of the head and I have seen mothers slap their daughters across the face. While I have never seen a dad punch his son or daughter, I have seen the results—both physical and emotional. Such actions in the midst of anger and frustration are most destructive to the parent/child relationship. Deep-seeded hurt and bitterness can result and may last a lifetime.

Give Only One Warning Regarding Discipline

Ultimately everyone benefits when the practice of giving only one warning is followed consistently. We have all heard parents say, "If you do that one more time…" and then the same statement is made over and over again, until finally some form of discipline happens.

One goal in parenting is to train children that they must obey the first time they are given instruction. They will learn the lesson quickly when they are told to do something and given a single warning—if they fail to obey, they will be disciplined. When a child learns that discipline will always be administered when the warning is ignored, he will soon practice first time obedience. Some will say such practice is unfair. What is truly unfair is the practice of warning over and over again and then finally disciplining in frustration. It is unfair because the child functions in continual uncertainty about when he must or must not obey. When discipline comes, it may very well be a harsh overreaction to the problem.

Never Threaten What You Will Not Do

"If you do that once more, you will never come shopping with me again."

Does anybody believe such foolish remarks? Not really, but parents make them all the time. Just listen the next time you are in the mall. The funny thing is that most kids would love it if they did not have to go shopping again; but they will be back out there the very next week. Appropriate "threats" are valid, but only if a parent intends to follow through.

Parents must think carefully about what will be a reasonable response to the disciplinary problem. When they conclude what would be right, they can make the threat and then MUST follow through. When children learn that their parents ALWAYS follow through on their threats, those same children will become very well behaved.

Do Not Bribe For Obedience, But Reward Good

"If you are good, I'll buy you a candy bar at the check-out counter."

Children must not obey because they are bribed to do so. What will the bribe have to be when they are 16—a new car? Children must be taught to obey, because mom and dad are in charge—period.

An unexpected reward for an obedient child is a great positive reinforcement to the whole training process. It is a simple expression of appreciation and encouragement that can go a long way in building great attitudes among the kids. Think through the difference between bribing and rewarding and then see the difference that can be made in the parent/child relationship.

Look for Opportunities to Compliment and Encourage

Parents are usually experts at identifying what their children do wrong. Sometimes children feel like that is all they ever hear from mom and dad. Start looking for the good things. Sure the bed should be made, dirty clothes should be put in the hamper, toys should be put away, but every person I know (young or old) is uplifted when someone takes notice of their efforts to do right. Children are especially encouraged when they feel like they are pleasing their parents.

A word of caution might be in order here. Be sure that when you compliment one, it is not to put down another. Playing children against one another only creates hurt and spite.

Do Not Tolerate Rebellion

Rebellion is unacceptable in the Christian home. Rebellion is the rejection of parental authority. Sometimes it is active, displaying itself through temper tantrums, direct disobedience, or verbal disrespect. Other times it is passive rebellion. The child acknowledges instruction, but perhaps "forgets" to do what he is told or finds some other way to ignore the assignment. Whether active or passive, some children find a way to let parents know that they will do what they want, when they want to do it.

The rejection of parental authority is actually the rejection of Divine authority. For instance, I used to tell my children that if they disobeyed a babysitter whom I put in charge, I would receive it as disobeying me. It is the Lord who puts parents in charge. To reject their authority is to reject God Himself. Rebellion must be conquered the first time it shows up in the life and attitude of a child.

Do Not Let Your Children Divide and Conquer

Parental agreement on standards and disciplinary procedures in the home is critical for success. Often, one parent believes in very strict standards, while the other may be less strict. The tendency will be for the less strict one to relax standards when the other parent is absent and for the stricter one to be all the more rule conscious when he or she is alone with the kids. I have heard words like "You may get away with that when I am away, but when I am here you will do it my way." Similarly, one parent may be harsher in discipline than the other; therefore, the one who is less harsh will tend to let things go by when he or she is alone. This common situation is not an easy one to resolve.

Let's first remember that strictness and harshness must not be equated with godliness or spiritual strength. Too many times someone will say of another, "He is a very strong godly man. He does not let his children do anything." As is addressed elsewhere in this book, strictness and harshness at times serve only to provoke a child to bitterness. Being the strictest parent in the church does not necessarily have any glory. On the other hand, we have all seen the destruction that results from undue permissiveness.

To find an agreeable balance is not easy, but when children see their parents divided on these issues, they will use the division to their own benefit. They will play on the parental emotion of the easier-going parent or pit the two parents against each other in discussion about what they might or might not be allowed to do. Parents must spend time talking and praying over standards and approaches to discipline. They may need to get counsel from their pastor or older couples who have already been down the parenting road. They must find a way to present to their children a unified front. Parental disagreement must be discussed in private, never in front of the children.

Do Not Punish Mistakes

We all make mistakes. For our children, it might be the tipping over of a glass of milk or knocking a lamp off a table. Now if they have been given instructions and they disobeyed, resulting in the accident, they may need to be disciplined in some way. If a parent says to not reach for a dish and the child spills the milk while reaching, that is disobedience. If the child is not disobeying and bumps his glass, that is a mistake. Those mistakes frustrate parents, but they are not worthy of discipline. I am so glad the Lord does not discipline us for our mistakes.

Apologize When You Fail Your Child

Too many parents think an apology to children would lower adults in the children's eyes. Just the opposite is true. Sometimes a promise of a special day out must be broken due to work or an emergency. Sometimes a parent punishes a child in error. Perhaps a child is proven to be innocent when he had been accused. "I'm sorry, will you forgive me?" will go a long way to encourage that little broken heart.

Never Display Temper—NEVER!

The Scriptures are loaded with warnings about temper. One of the most challenging is Proverbs 14:29, which states, *"He that is slow to wrath is of great understanding: but he that is hasty of spirit exalteth folly."* When we display temper, we say things and do things that may be regretted for a long time. Apologies are always in order for such behavior—but like it or not, deep wounds from a parent to a child heal slowly and sometimes fester for years, affecting the child's attitudes in their own marriage and parenting experience.

Parents seem to think that yelling, slamming doors, and similar tactics of intimidation will bring the desired results in kids. Our goal in discipline, however, is not to create fear in our children, but to continue their training in how to live and at the same time point them to the Lord. A time of discipline must be a spiritual time. Let me say that again. A time of discipline must be a spiritual time. Uncontrolled anger is a detriment to parenting and child rearing. In James 1:20, we read, *"For the wrath of man worketh not the righteousness of God."* If we lose our temper with our children, we shut God out of the training process.

Make Discipline a Spiritual Time

In the last paragraph we stated that a time of discipline must be a spiritual time. Indeed it must, but we must conscientiously make it so. It would be nice if children were bad at just the right time, but they do wrong when it is most inconvenient for parents. Little Susie throws a tantrum just when the new neighbor stops by for a visit or Billy defies the instruction to go to the car when dad is leaving church and chatting with the pastor at the door.

Consequently, parental frustration, embarrassment, and impatience can all enter into the time of correction. It would be so much easier if they would do such things when no one was around and we had convenient time to stop what we were doing to calmly address the matter. It is at these times we must remember that discipline is not intended as a time to relieve our frustration or save face in front of others. The discipline is for the long term benefit of our child. To succeed spiritually, it will have to be a quiet time of discussion about the wrong that has been done. The discussion should be designed to bring confession of the wrong; acknowledgment that the wrong was sin and therefore an offense to God, as well as to the parent; and appropriate discipline to reinforce the correction. Prayer with the child can be very important in making it a spiritual time, but praying would be a mockery if it follows parental displays of temper.

Do Not Compare Your Child Unfavorably

"Why can't you be like your brother?"

This is not an uncommon statement, but it is valueless in discipline. Your little guy may not care much for his brother, so why would he want to be like him? And if he does love his brother, he will soon despise him because of the constant unfavorable comparisons. We should use only one measuring rod with our children and that is what God wants them to be. Let them—in fact, help them to stand or fall before the Lord and His Word.

I observed a father and his son on one occasion. The boy was giving every ounce of strength and effort he had to please his dad on an athletic field. Later the father commented very favorably about another boy and said, "Now that's the kind of boy I want to have." What a tragedy! The other boy may have been more capable of performing athletically, but he was being held up as worthy of love and appreciation because of his skills on a field of competition. He may or may not have been doing his best and underneath his skills may have been no heart for God, but he became the measuring rod for the man's son.

Our children may not be equipped to perform athletically, academically, or artfully. If they are, they should do their best and use their skills for God's glory. Thankfully however, the things that matter most are the things that are available to all. The tender heart and surrendered life are the things parents should encourage. In those areas everyone has the opportunity to equally achieve and experience success.

Guard Your Words—Do Not Belittle Your Child or Call Him Names

"You are a mess; you are a brat; you make me sick; I wish I had never had you."

Words can hurt deeply. The greatest hurts come from those whom we need as encouragers. May the Lord help us to never make these kinds of insensitive remarks to the precious little ones entrusted to our care by the Lord.

Do you remember the saying, "Sticks and stones may break my bones, but names (words) will never hurt me"? Many of us, when we were kids, used that saying as a feeble defense against someone who was tearing us apart with unkind remarks. The truth is, those words cut deeply and left us with far greater and longer lasting pain than any stick or stone. Parents must not do that kind of damage to their children. Proverbs 12:18 reads, *"There is that spea-*

keth like the piercings of a sword..." The verse continues, *"...but the tongue of the wise is health."* Please think carefully before you rebuke your child. Don't say things to demean his character. Address what he did wrong and correct him, but don't wound his spirit in your moment of anger and frustration. Proverbs 18:14 states, *"The spirit of a man will sustain his infirmity; but a wounded spirit who can bear."*

Teach Your Child
That Ultimately He Answers to the Lord

In one conference, I was asked if it would be appropriate to discipline all the children, if there was no success in determining which one had done wrong. I knew how that parent must feel, because when my children were little and something was done, I wanted to know who did it. I could find little rest in my soul until I had been able to find the culprit. I can remember many times gathering my five together and asking, "Who did it?" Of course, they all denied being the guilty party. I would go down the row asking each one, "Did you do it?" At times, all five would deny their guilt. I would say, "Well somebody did it and it was not me, nor was it your mother, so it had to be one of you." After working them through that bit of logic, I would go down the row again with the same question, "Did you do it?" I often heard "No" five times. I would then send them all to their rooms to think about it and told them we would regather shortly. The results were the same. Then I would try to read their faces to see if I could figure out who looked guilty. Sometimes one would finally admit his guilt, or one might tell on another.

I learned along the way, however, that in those times I needed to teach them a lesson that was far more important then my succeeding in my detective work. The lesson was a simple one. Dad might never find out who did the wrong, but an omniscient God in heaven knows all and, therefore, catches us every time. I realized that this truth was a critical one for them to learn because I would not always be there. He would! I wanted them to know that ultimately they answer to the Lord, not me. I hope they will carry that truth with them all their earthly days. If they do, they will be faithful servants of God all their life. Work hard to build this lesson into your little ones—it will pay rich dividends for years to come.

Conclusion

Successful parenting calls for the use of certain skills and practices. They are not secrets, hidden away somewhere in the intellect of a select few. They are guidelines based on direct biblical teaching, application of biblical principles, and a good mix of God-given common sense.

One of the great things about the Bible is that its teachings work. It is not a book given only to reveal the person and character of God or only to unfold His plan of redemption. In the midst of those unfathomable truths, a host of God-given guidelines are found for how to live our day-to-day earthly experience. Those guidelines are as inspired as every other truth in the Bible. It is God's desire that His people raise up many godly generations in succession. It has not happened in years gone by. It can happen in your family, but only if you carefully and faithfully follow scriptural teaching.

6 BALANCE IN DISCIPLINE & TRAINING

The Relationship between Love and Control

A long time ago I was introduced to the chart below. I do not know who first developed it, but I think I saw it at an Institute In Basic Youth Conflicts seminar back in the 70s. The message is quite simple, but extremely important.

```
                    100% | Love
                         |
    Permissiveness       |        Authoritativeness
                         |
                         |
 0% ─────────────────────┼───────────────────── 100%
                         |                    Control
                         |
       Neglect           |        Authoritarianism
                         |
                     0%  |
```

The two intersecting lines represent degrees of love and control in the experience of child training. The vertical line represents love. The lower end of the graph portrays very little love. The top end of the graph portrays a great deal of love. The horizontal line represents control of our children. The left side of the graph portrays very little control. The right side of the graph portrays a great deal of control. As the two lines intersect they form 4 quadrants, suggesting four experiences in parenting.

The bottom left quadrant is defined by very little love and very little control. Imagine a child growing up in such a setting. He is left by himself for long periods of time, with no rules or standards to guide him. He can do what he wants, go where he wants, and associate with whomever he chooses. He knows little of parental love and care. He becomes a survivor, doing whatever he needs to do to get by. He may easily become a victim of an adult or older young person, ending up physically, sexually, emotionally, or mentally abused. What he misses in family life, he may seek to substitute with the wrong kind of friends. He is easily tempted and may take up habits involving tobacco, drugs, or alcohol. It would not be unusual for him to find companionship in a gang setting, which might only lead to greater problems and sometimes participation in crime. He is suffering from *neglect*. With 25% of young people growing up in broken homes and about 70% of all women going out to work everyday, many children are growing up neglected.

***

The bottom right quadrant is defined by very little love, but much control. The child in this setting does not lack rules and standards, but enforcement is carried out with little or no love. This is a prescription for disaster. The *authoritarianism* in this home demands absolute obedience to parental authority, but the accompanying tension is what dominates the atmosphere of the family.

Rules are established for the parent's convenience, not as a framework for molding the child's character, training him how to live an orderly life, or how get along with others. In such a home, discipline of the children may be harsh and unfair, while compassion and understanding are nowhere to be found.

As Christians, we must be careful to reject such a home life. We should have high standards of conduct in our homes and require obedience to the rules, but if an atmosphere of tension or fear is created, the home will fail miserably. Home life should be based on scriptural directives and principles making the Christian home far different from its worldly counterpart. But if that same home does not overflow with love, children will reject the very things parents seek to teach.

Harsh and unfair discipline can often lead to bitterness among children, as they perceive they have not been treated properly. In such a home, a "do as I say, not as I do" mentality can cause a child to reject hypocritical parents and the faith those parents profess. The child in this home is anxious to get out. This in turn may bring on greater tragedy in years to come. Young men may leave home before they are ready, with a determination to never return. Later when they need counsel, they will hesitate to turn to the parents, whom they resent from younger years. Young ladies, in their desire to get out of the home, may marry the wrong man and regret it for the rest of their lives.

Autocratic rule is efficient, but it does not build love, trust, and genuine respect. At the root of its failure in parenting, and every other realm of authority, is its neglect of the Lord, as the One who gives authority. Let us never forget we are accountable to Him for how we treat those He has entrusted to our care.

***

The upper left quadrant of the graph is defined by a lot of love, but not much control. While this approach to parenting is favored above the previous two options, the Bible in no way supports *permissiveness* as an acceptable alternative. Much love is to be applauded. May children never doubt the love of their parents.

A comment I have heard too often comes from people who experienced little love growing up. They say something like "I know my father loved me, but he never told me." Do not let your children grow up with that kind of testimony. It would be tragic if parents had to be encouraged to love their children. Sometimes that is the case, but more often parents need encouragement to express their love. Children need to be hugged and kissed from the moment they are born, and those expressions of affection need never end. Children also benefit from being told they are loved. Tell them a dozen times a day.

Love alone, however, is not sufficient to produce God-honoring, parent-respecting, faithful children. Today, one of the greatest problems is that children are out of control. You will see the problem manifested at the local mall, church, or family room.

The Bible is filled with warnings regarding children who are out of control. The Bible teaches that a man is unfit for pastoral ministry if his children are not in subjection to his authority. Proverbs 13:24 warns that the parent who spares the rod actually hates his son, but the parent who loves his son will chasten him betimes. *Betimes* means early, diligently, so as to keep him from getting out of control. The Old Testament priest, Eli, was judged because he did not restrain his sons from doing evil.

Never has there been so little respect for authority, as there is in our generation. Permissiveness will bring greater success than authoritarianism or neglect, but the Bible teaches us a better way.

***

The upper right quadrant of the graph is defined by a lot of love and much control. *Authoritativeness* will hold high standards and require due submission to authority, but it is balanced by love, compassion and understanding.

The parent, who carries out his duties in this way, manifests an understanding of his own accountability to the Lord for the child that has been given to him. He recognizes the obligation of parenting to train up a child in the way he should go. He puts emphasis on obedience to and respect for authority. He seeks to mold the child's character, but realizes that the child may need to see Christ in the life of his parent, before he will take Christ as his own Savior. Children raised in an authoritative setting are most likely to love and respect their parents, to adopt their parents' standards and values, and to follow their parents' faith.

Striking the balance is not easy, but we must strive to attain it. Children need to know the standards of the home and fully understand what is expected of them. They need to be treated justly. They need understanding of their maturity level, of the limits of their talents and abilities, and of their special needs. With due consideration of each child's unique character and personality, training and discipline must be consistent. Children need to be taught how to evaluate right and wrong, good and bad, and true and false so they can develop convictions and discernment as they mature. In the midst of that training, they must be showered with expressions of genuine love, demonstrating an acceptance of who they are as individual creations of God. Challenged to be their best for Him, such children will be a blessing to their parents and to all others who look on.

The Relationship between Authority and Influence

Parents must be aware of the relationship between *authority* and *influence*. Everyone should submit appropriately to various realms of authority including the Lord Himself, government, church, employers, husbands, parents, and others to whom authority may be delegated.

The Lord has given primary and direct authority over a child to his parents. Children are told in a number of places in Scripture to obey their parents. It is assumed the child's response to other authorities will be in accordance with parental training and instruction. Parents tell their children what to do and when to do it. The wise parent will recognize, however, that parental control will gradually diminish as the child grows toward adulthood. This does not mean that parents are not responsible for their children as they grow and move through the teen years. It does mean that parents, having provided good training, will gradually entrust more and more decisions to their maturing child.

Consider a simple illustration of food and clothing: Mom picks out the clothes a small child will wear on a given day. Eventually the child will make that choice, within parental guidelines. Meals are prepared for small children with minimal concern for what they might want on a given day. Eventually the child might be asked about preferences. As the child grows up, more and more choices are his to make and those choices will involve more and more serious areas of life. In time, parents will relinquish all authority over the child and will become a counselor and friend to the young adult they have reared and trained. As the young person steps out on his own, the success of parental training will be revealed.

What may very well make the difference, in the life of a child, are the influences that have impacted him during his years of growing up in his home. The exercise of authority may win the battle of a particular day, but authority alone will not produce a godly young person. From early on, the child is affected by many influences. Some of them will be good, but some of them will be bad. While authority primarily appeals to the conscience and will of a child, influences appeal to the mind, emotions, and curiosity. The successful parent will seek to carry out authority in a proper way, but will also seek to be the greatest earthly influence in his child's life. When all is said and done, influences may have a far greater effect on the child than mere parental authority.

Billy is seven years old when a neighbor child invites him to attend the local theater to see a new and exciting movie. His dad, as a godly Christian with good standards, denies Billy the opportunity to go. He is in charge of Billy and must maintain a good testimony. While Billy's dad has properly exercised his authority, another force has immediately come into play—influence. Billy's friend, Bobby, when told that Billy cannot go to see the movie, immediately informs Billy that his dad is mean. He also tells him that nothing is wrong with going to the movie theater. When Bobby returns from seeing the movie, he tells Billy how great it was and how much fun he had. Billy offers a mild complaint to his dad, but knows he had no choice but to obey. Billy struggles, however, because many of his friends attend the movies and they say it is great. They do not seem to be hurt by going. Billy wonders what it is like to go to the movies and really wishes he could go at least once. The battle for Billy's heart has only just begun.

As the years go on, many more issues will be raised in Billy's life—clothes, music, friendships, activities, church attendance, respect for others, attitudes, curfews, appropriate conversation, appearance, places to go, moral issues, and a host of others. In dealing with each one, dad and mom will have authority to control Billy and define what is acceptable. During those same years, however, Billy will be impacted by a variety of influences that will vie for his heart. As already mentioned, some of them will be good, while some will be bad.

The Word of God instructs us about influences in numerous places. Think about these words:

> *"Blessed is the man that walketh not in the counsel of the ungodly, nor standeth in the way of sinners, nor sitteth in the seat of the scornful." (Psalm 1:1)*

> *"I will set no wicked thing before mine eyes..." (Psalm 101:3)*

> *"My son, if sinners entice thee, consent thou not." (Proverbs 1:10)*

> *"He that walketh with wise men shall be wise: but a companion of fools shall be destroyed." (Proverbs 13:20)*

> *"Cease, my son, to hear the instruction that causeth to err from the words of knowledge." (Proverbs 19:27)*

> *"Make no friendship with an angry man; and with a furious man thou shalt not go: lest thou learn his ways, and get a snare to thy soul." (Proverbs 22:24–25)*

> *"For by wise counsel thou shalt make thy war: and in the multitude of counsellors there is safety." (Proverbs 24:6)*

> *"Iron sharpeneth iron; so a man sharpeneth the countenance of his friend." (Proverbs 27:17)*

> *"...he that is a companion of riotous men shameth his father." (Proverbs 28:7b)*

> *"Thus saith the Lord, Learn not the way of the heathen..." (Jeremiah 10:2a)*

What influences will affect your child?

The Friends They Make — Everyone has friends. Some friends provide spiritual encouragement and blessing, but others may only tend to bring a person down. Your child will have friends. To some degree you will be able to control who his friends are and how much time he will spend under their influence. As time goes on, you will have less control. Parents much teach their children what the Bible says about friends.

The Television They Watch — Most people watch television. Keep in mind that every television program has an agenda. It is trying to influence the way you think. It is attempting to affect your values. If you are influenced by it, how much more will your child be affected by what he sees and hears?

The Members of Their Family — One would hope that family would be supportive of godly values and godly living. That is not always the case. Some relatives are not saved; and some profess to be saved, but do not live for the Lord. It is hard to escape the influence of family. We cannot isolate our children from family members who advocate different views from ours, but we must be aware of the impact they can have on our little ones.

The Experiences They Have at Church — No perfect church exists, so stop hoping you will find one. Serve in a church where the Word of God is faithfully preached and the pastor is a man of integrity. Worship in a setting where the values of your home are supported and your children are taught to surrender all to the Lord. Your faithfulness in church will help your children recognize how important living for the Lord is to you. Unfaithfulness will convince them that worship in church is just a matter of convenience, not conviction. If we want our children to be positively influenced by church, we will have to demonstrate it is high on our list of priorities.

The Scriptures — The Word of God must be given a place of prominence in family life, if we want our children to be properly influenced by it. If the Bible is only opened when we are in church, it will mean little to our children. They must see that we depend on Scripture to guide us. We read it, memorize it, and meditate on it daily.

The Education They Receive — Our children spend hundreds of hours per year in a formal educational setting. Teachers are held in high esteem and the instruction given in the classroom will mold the minds and affect the hearts of the students. Curricula along with rules and standards will vary from school to school. Fellow students' attitudes and actions will have bearing on your child. Every parent must be involved in the education of the child: knowing what is being taught, who is doing the teaching, and what philosophies undergird the whole program. Educational options are available to most parents today, and each has potential strengths and weaknesses. The educational program selected for your child will have a major influence on him as he learns and matures.

The Material They Read — Whether it be the Word of God, a take-home paper from Sunday School, a novel, textbook, comic book, or a billboard—what a child reads will affect his mind and imagination, peek his curiosity, and stir his emotions. Provide him with the best of reading materials, because out of them may come his hopes and desires for the future.

The Music They Hear — Music has a message even if there are no lyrics. It is a deaf man who thinks music is amoral. Watch a young child of one or two years of age, as they respond to the music they hear. For the rest of their lives they will be affected by music. Some of it will lift their hearts to God, while some may appeal to their basest desires.

The Leaders Over Them — Leaders in school, church, athletic and fine arts programs, clubs, or the nation can inspire people to great vision and action. Parents must make sure they know what direction the leaders over their children are going. Leaders can become our heroes. A child's hero may influence the pattern of his whole life.

The Guests in Their Home — Home is a sacred place in many ways. It should provide a godly atmosphere. Children will be influenced by the conversation at a dinner table or out on the deck. A wise parent will bring servants of the Lord to their home, whether the pastor, visiting speakers, or missionaries, and will allow the children to sit and listen to stories telling of the faithfulness of the Lord.

The Atmosphere of Their Home — Walk into some homes and you are immediately impressed with the warmth of Christianity. Conversation honors the Lord. Plaques on the wall point one to Christ. Music playing magnifies the Savior. Other homes are cold and uninviting. The home should be a haven of rest where parents and children alike find spiritual refreshment.

The Standards of Their Home — Having respect for authority, being mannerly in words and conversation, being courteous, and many other qualities will be developed, not because a child is ordered to act a certain way, but because he grows up in the midst of a decent and respectable family life. He observes what is right and how to treat others. He adopts that way of life as his own. On the other hand, children reared in a home without good standards will often be ill-mannered and impolite. They usually do not know any better—it is just due to the influence of their own home.

The Culture of Our Society — The pierced ear and nose, long hair or short, pleated pants or straight, mini skirts or maxi skirts, high heels or low heels, what is in and what is out, styles and trends. All of these things and so much more are a testimony to the powerful influence of an ever-changing culture.

Much of it is related to commercialism and the desire for the dollar. I have never minded the trendsetters trying to lure people into buying the latest style. I just marvel that the public follows along like dumb sheep, feeling the need to keep buying every new thing that is set before them. I am sure you know children are greatly influenced by our culture and not just in regards to fashion. Views on family, marriage, personal responsibility, and life itself are ever changing and those degenerating views of fallen man are finding acceptance among many who name the name of Christ.

The Parents God Gave Them — Parents must not only exercise authority over their children, they must govern, as much as possible, the influences that come into their children's lives. Even more importantly, they must work hard at being the people of greatest influence in their children's lives. Some parents control their children outwardly, so the children are forced to do right in their early years at home. At the same time, those parents may have very little positive influence in the development of the children's values, feelings, and views. It breaks my heart when I hear of teens making statements like "As soon as I am 18, I am getting out of here so I can do what I want to do." In Proverbs 23:26 we read, *"My son, give me thine heart, and let thine eyes observe my ways."* Here was a dad who went beyond the mere exercise of parental authority. He wanted to have great influence in the life of his son, to show him how to live in a godly way. Proverbs 20:7 states, *"The just man walketh in his integrity: his children are blessed after him."* This text tells of the great influence a man of integrity can have on his child. Let a man be a hypocrite and his child will reap accordingly. Remember Proverbs 17:6b—*"...The glory of children are their fathers."* A child is ready to learn from his dad, because he glories in him. He loves his dad from day one. He wants to be near him. He wants to spend time with him. God's intent is that dads and moms might have great influence in their children's lives. If only parents would see the importance of influence being a ready companion of authority.

Balance is a great word and sometimes parenting seems like a balancing act. How important it is, however, to invest the necessary time and energy into the lives of our children. Sometimes when our children are little a day can seem long; but at the same time, the years rush by. How quickly the time passes and our children are grown, never to return to the same relationship we had when they were little. As children grow into adulthood, parents do not want to carry regrets over what they should have done. They want to rejoice as they see their children serve the Lord and begin the task of rearing their own little ones. We must do it right—we only get one chance.

7 SOME PRACTICAL THOUGHTS

The Scriptures give some very grave warnings to remind parents of the seriousness of their task. Often people ask if a parent can be held responsible for what a child does when he is 30 or 40 years old. Thankfully, the answer—to a large degree—is no. A person cannot go through life blaming his sins on the failures of his parents. The child must accept responsibility for his own actions at some point in life. The wise parent, however, will remember that to some degree, his child will forever reflect his home life.

For instance, Colossians 3:21 says, *"Fathers, provoke not your children to anger, lest they be discouraged."* The term *discouraged* means to be disheartened. I describe it as killing the spirit of the child. His desire to please and to help is destroyed by a father who forever criticizes every effort made by the child—nothing is ever good enough. When he paints the fence, he misses too many places. When he washes the car, he leaves too many spots. No matter how hard he tries, there is always criticism with little appreciation. Soon the child stops trying. Mediocrity in every task becomes acceptable to him, because appreciation was never shown for greater effort. Excitement over a project is never shown, because criticism always destroyed enthusiasm in years gone by. The child with this kind of experience growing up may very well carry his discouragement into adulthood and it will affect his whole life.

Should he carry hurt and anger into adulthood? No! Should he forgive, put it all behind him, and go on to be all that he can be for Christ? Yes! Will he? Maybe not. Is he responsible? Yes. Is he reflecting his home life? Yes. You may know this young man we've just described. His father is a very successful, sharp, business man, but you have wondered how he could have such a dud for a son. Let's look at some scriptures and consider some very practical matters in handling our children.

Provoke Not Your Children

We live in a world that loves positives and seems to despise negatives of any kind. Negatives, however, are powerful motivators in every circumstance. One must always do certain things, which are balanced by the things one must not do. When it comes to parenting, a balance must be maintained to bring success. The warning to provoke not your children is found in two places in Scripture. Ephesians 6:4 reads, *"And, ye fathers, provoke not your children to wrath: but bring them up in the nurture and admonition of the Lord."* Colossians 3:21, as noted above, states, *"Fathers, provoke not your children to anger, lest they be discouraged."* Let's examine these two texts and make application of them to a few situations.

Provoke Not Your Children to Wrath
Ephesians 6:4

This text is discussed in an earlier chapter, but to review it and enlarge the discussion here may be helpful. To receive the full impact of the warning of Ephesians 6:4, it is necessary to go back to the beginning of the context in which it is found. Ephesians 6:1 begins, *"Children, obey your parents in the Lord: for this is right."* Children are under the authority of their parents and are clearly instructed to obey, because it is the right thing to do. After exhorting the children and showing them special promises from the Lord for those who honor their parents, the Apostle Paul then instructs the father. It is as if he says, "Hey dad, I just told your children to obey you, now I want to tell you something. Make sure you do not provoke your children to wrath." It is a reminder that parental authority is not absolute authority. Parents are in charge of their children to represent the Lord, who gave the children to them in the first place.

What does it mean to provoke a child to wrath? The key to understanding the challenge is in the word *provoke*. To use "provoke" shows that this is not a warning against godly standards or parental strictness, for those things in themselves do not create provocation. In being told to not provoke their children, parents are warned about those words, attitudes, and actions that can exasperate and frustrate a child, bringing him to the point of bitterness and wrath. Abusive language, displays of temper, unrelenting teasing, inappropriate discipline, and inconsistent rules can all bring a child to great frustration. Parents will be most sensitive to the danger of these practices when they remember that their children have been entrusted to them by the gracious hand of the Lord.

Should children obey their parents? Yes! However, parents will hopefully value obedience that is rooted in loving respect from their children, rather than the fear of punishment. Name calling, yelling, uncontrolled anger, and parental inconsistencies may not result in the forfeiture of obedience, but over a number of years may result in the loss of a loving parent/child relationship.

Let me offer an illustration that occurs in many families. Imagine dad going to work one day and being called into his superior's office. Compliments are given and dad receives a promotion and a nice raise. That afternoon, as he arrives home, he sees his son's bicycle parked on the sidewalk. He has instructed his son on numerous occasions that the bike is to be put away. On this day, however, dad is in a great mood. As he enters the house, he says nothing about the bike because he is happy and having a wonderful day. During work the next day, he is called back to his superior's office. A terrible mistake has been made. The promotion and raise were never intended; in fact, dad is on the lay off list in light of a company merger. Dad heads for home and, sure enough, as he arrives, the bike is on the walkway again. This time upon entering the house dad blows his stack, punishes his son, and reminds him with great anger how many times he has been told about that bike. All would agree the bike should not have been left on the sidewalk, but if (as in this case) discipline is administered based on dad's mood rather than based on the family rules, a hurt and bitter son may be the result.

Provoke Not Your Children Lest They Get Discouraged
Colossians 3:21

This warning to parents is very similar to the one just considered. The King James Version includes the phrase *to anger*, which is given in italics, suggesting these two words are not included in the original text. The concept of provocation is the same as addressed in the previous section. The warning here, from the Colossians text, is *"lest they (the children) be discouraged."* To be "discouraged" means to be disheartened. It suggests the killing of the spirit or attitude of a child.

Again we can illustrate from a common family experience. It is appropriate for a child to have chore assignments around the house. Those assignments can range from the simple task of putting their dirty clothes in the hamper to the more challenging responsibility of mowing the grass. Not too much is involved with putting clothes in the hamper, but mowing the grass could involve handling gasoline and oil, using the mower, trimming edges, cleaning the mower, and properly putting everything away. It would be common for a piece of clothing to end up on the floor, instead of in the hamper. That could be a bother to a parent, but far more frustrating would be a child's careless handling of mowing the lawn. The response to a child's failure to do a task exactly right will make the difference in the child's continuing attitudes toward his responsibilities and toward his parents. Too often, a little grass left on the sidewalk or a few spots untrimmed can become a major area of conflict. Appreciation for a job well done, though not perfectly done, will go a long way in providing motivation to do even better next time. Extreme criticism for a few errors can kill the spirit of a child. As soon as a father convinces his son that his efforts will never be good enough, he will foster a spirit of discouragement and defeatism that may never be reversed. Skillful, loving parenting will offer a "thank you" for the task performed and inspiration to try a little harder next time. In many conferences, I have talked to people who grew up convinced that they could never do enough to please their parents, no matter how hard they tried.

Exhort, Comfort, and Charge
I Thessalonians 2:11

In this text Paul wrote, *"As ye know how we exhorted and comforted and charged every one of you, as a father doth his children..."* Paul is likening his ministry to the believers of Thessalonica to that of a father working with his child. This is an important concept for every father. Paul said he exhorted, comforted, and charged. If a dad can grasp these methods of dealing with his children, he can be more certain of success in rearing them.

To exhort is to encourage. It is to motivate and urge another to keep trying. "You can do it; don't quit" is the message. While there is deeper meaning, to be sure, the exhorter is somewhat of a cheerleader who knows the person on the playing field must perform the task at hand—but who also realizes the value of inspiring them on to success. Dads and moms need to be their children's best cheerleaders. It is not unusual to see a parent literally cheering on a child in athletic competition, but it needs to be seen more in the daily routine of life. Children need to be encouraged in spiritual matters, handling problems, serving the Lord, witnessing to others, working hard at school, learning verses for Sunday School, and carrying out responsibilities at home. They need parents who are standing by with words of exhortation. They need someone to encourage them on to spiritual, academic, and social success. The term *exhort* is a prospective term; that is, it always looks to the future. It is a word that inspires confidence and hope for success.

The next term Paul used was *comfort*. *To comfort* is to console. Sometimes our children give their best and don't succeed to the degree they would desire. The cheerleader now becomes the comforter. A child needs to know it is okay to come in second, if they have done their best for the Lord. Not everybody gets all "A's" on their report card; not everybody passes their driver's test the first time; not everybody makes first chair in the orchestra. Parents need to be there to affirm their love to their children when defeat has come. They need to help them get motivated to try again. The word *comfort* literally means "near speech." It speaks of someone who comes closely to another, to counsel and console with soothing, tender words. Sometimes parents are unnecessarily hard on their children. Second best to some is never acceptable.

I remember a young lady a few years back, who was expected to win the gold medal in figure skating at the Olympic competition. She got the silver medal instead. When she was being interviewed she was asked, "How does it feel to have lost the gold medal?" Her reply was great. She said, "I did not lose the gold medal. I won the silver medal." What wonderful perspective! Thousands of young people skate and never make an Olympic team. She had made the team and was judged to be the second best skater in the whole world. Some could only see that she had not been judged to be the best. Too often parents treat their children as if only first place will gain their acceptance and approval. Children need to be assured that it's okay to fall, as long as you don't stay down. Kids won't stay down, if they find a parent's hand to help lift them up.

The last term Paul used in this text was *charged*. *To charge* is to summon as a witness. The charge was based on Paul's own words, actions, and life. In verse 10 he said, *"Ye are our witnesses...how holily and justly and unblameably we behaved ourselves among you that believe."* In verse 12 he says, *"That ye would walk worthy of God..."* His point is clear—he was challenging his readers to walk worthy of God and he charged them (summoned them as witnesses) to acknowledge that he had lived a faithful example before them. He was asking them to do as he did, not simply do what he said. His challenge was spiritual—*"to walk worthy of God."* That was significant because spiritual victory is equally available to all. Not all can play the trumpet or succeed athletically, but all can serve the Lord with a tender heart. Dads and moms need to get their own priorities right, so they can help their children be successful in the things that really matter.

Children may experience great frustration in life, because they will want to do things at which they will be unable to succeed. They may spend hours crying, because they could not make a starting position on some team. If their success in making that team is as important to their parents as it is to them, the whole family is in trouble. They need someone to tell them that the team is not all that important. Other things matter more. Teaching and learning this is not easy because we live in a very mixed up world. We tend to get swept away in the world's system of values. The world praises and rewards athletic ability, physical beauty, intelligence, etc., but only a relatively small number of people are so endowed.

God praises and rewards the surrendered life. When Paul charged the believers at Thessalonica, he was telling them to observe that his words, actions, and life demonstrated success in the things that really mattered. He wanted them to enjoy that same success. Help your children understand what really matters in this world. Then exhort them, comfort them, and charge them as they strive for spiritual mastery.

Every Child is Different

The last section alluded to the fact that every child is different. Every parent must recognize and accept this significant truth. Psalm 103:13-14 has many important applications, but we will introduce one here. The Psalmist wrote, *"Like as a father pitieth his children, so the Lord pitieth them that fear him. For he knoweth our frame; he remembereth that we are dust."* The key to getting the meaning of the text is understanding what it means *to pity*. The English word normally suggests compassion toward one who suffers. The Hebrew term suggests understanding and compassion from the Lord relating to the specific frailties we experience as humans because *"we are dust."*

To pity further suggests that fathers are to have understanding and compassion toward their children, because they are children. Parents need to remember that each child matures gradually and that each child is different from his peers. Even twin brothers may have totally different interests as they grow up. One may enjoy athletics, and one may not. Hopefully the worth of a child to his parents will not be dependent on his athletic skill and interest. If it is not athletics, it may be hunting, fishing, fine arts, academics, mechanics, cooking, sewing, or any number of other areas. Sometimes parents are trying to live their unfulfilled dreams through their children. Sometimes they demand their children enjoy and participate in activities that the parents enjoy. Without a doubt, children should be encouraged to try new activities and learn new skills; however, the skill level attained or the interest shown in an activity must never be the basis for a child's acceptance or rejection by his parents.

No Favorites

A great source of turmoil and tension in the home is the practice of favoring one child above the others. Genesis 37:3-4 reads *"Now Israel loved Joseph more than all his children, because he was the son of his old age...And when his brethren saw that their father loved him more than all his brethren, they hated him, and could not speak peaceably unto him."* I am absolutely amazed at Israel (Jacob), because he grew up with favoritism in his family. His father Isaac loved Esau more than Jacob, because Esau was an outdoors man and Isaac loved to eat the venison that Esau killed (Genesis 25:28). How hard it must have been for Jacob growing up—but then he committed the very same sin against his own children. The results were tragic as the brothers of Joseph hated him because he was the favorite. Esau was his father's favorite because Esau was a hunter. Joseph was his father's favorite because he was the son of his old age.

I have seen children be the favorite because they were the oldest, or they looked like a particular parent, or they followed in a parent's footsteps in liking a particular activity or entering a particular vocation. Favoritism only brings disaster. For Jacob it inspired deception; for Joseph it brought hatred. In your family it can bring heartache, too. Everyone recognizes a favorite and everyone suffers because of it.

8 RECOGNIZING THE DISTINCTION BETWEEN MOM'S & DAD'S ROLE

When children are addressed in Scripture, they are consistently told to obey their parents and to honor both father and mother. This instruction demonstrates why parents must function in as much agreement as possible when setting rules and standards for the home. Children must not be allowed to work parents against one another by taking advantage of parental disagreement; nor must children be caught between a dad and mom who approach rules and discipline differently.

While children (who are under parental authority) must submit to both parents, Scripture clearly indicates that the Lord distinguishes between the role of each parent in the training and discipline process.

Mom's Role

Let's consider the couple of texts that speak to the child and his obedience to his mother.

> *"My son, hear the instruction of thy father, and forsake not the law of thy mother." (Proverbs 1:8)*

> *"My son, keep thy father's commandment, and forsake not the law of thy mother." (Proverbs 6:20)*

Notice that in each case the specific frame of reference for the child's obedience to mom is always her law. In these two examples, two realms of dad's authority are mentioned, namely his instruction and his commandment. We will come back to those later in this discussion, but for now let's consider the *"law of thy mother."*

The Hebrew term *Torah* translated "law" is the most common term for law in the Old Testament. The term used in its technical sense is the name given to the complete body of Jewish religious law. Obviously, it is not the technical sense of the term that is used here. The general use of the term means a statute or a precept—in other words, rules and standards. We get more help understanding this term by going to the root word of *torah*, which is *yarah*. *Yarah* is related to teaching and directing, as if to throw or shoot an arrow. It can mean "to point out" and, interestingly, suggests the idea of "aiming the finger."

Considering all these ideas helps us form an understanding of mom's role in parenting. Mom sets up rules and standards for the household and the children are to obey them. She may even aim her finger at her child to impress upon him the seriousness of the standard she has set for her home. In every well-run Christian home, rules of conduct exist and generally mom establishes them. Some language is acceptable, and some is not. Everything has a place and everything should be in its place. Dirty clothes go in the hamper, feet stay off the furniture, good manners are taught and required, lights are turned off when one leaves a room, hats come off when the house is entered, and hands are washed before eating. Moms may be heard to say such things as: Leave your boots outside; cover your mouth when you cough; do not put your dirty hands on the wall; and be sure to make your bed before you come to breakfast. Mom is the keeper of the house and she builds her household through a system of standards. Children are to obey the law of their mother. This concept does not eliminate mom from some of the broader responsibilities of parenting, but clearly identifies a realm of responsibility that is biblically assigned to her. Dad should be a supporter and, when necessary, an enforcer of the standards. As a matter of fact, he might do well to follow the rules, too.

Dad's Role

Compare *"law of thy mother"* with the realms of authority and responsibility that are assigned to dad. We noted briefly that Proverbs 1:8 spoke of the *"instruction of thy father"* and Proverbs 6:20 spoke of the *"commandment of thy father."* Consider other texts:

> *"For I give you good doctrine, forsake ye not my law." (Proverbs 4:2)*

> *"My son, attend unto my words; incline thine ear unto my sayings." (Proverbs 4:20)*

> *"My son, attend unto my wisdom, and bow thine ear to my understanding." (Proverbs 5:1)*

These and other texts reveal a very broad realm of responsibility for dad. He holds a primary role in the training and discipline of the children God entrusts to him.

First, we will take note that Proverbs 4:2 suggests that dad will also have laws, rules, and standards which he will set for the children. They will not conflict with mom's rules, but may relate to areas of dad's concern. Perhaps dad declares no child is ever to hit a sibling, there is an appropriate way to answer the telephone, or no one uses the computer without specific permission. In the verse dealing with dad's law is the statement from father to son, *"I give you good doctrine." Doctrine* is teaching and the use of the term in this verse may emphasize the idea that dad's laws are to be supported by good teaching. Dad does not simply "lay down the law," he teaches why the rule exists.

Proverbs 1:8 tells the child to hear the instruction of the father. *Instruction* suggests warning, reproof, chastisement, and correction. Mom may certainly correct or warn a child in a given situation, but dad needs to see that in the broader experience of parenting, instruction is his role.

Too often the discipline of children is left in mom's hands, because she generally has more time with the children. Her discipline, however, should be seen as extension of dad's role as head and leader of the home.

Proverbs 6:20 tells the child to keep the commandment of the father. *To keep* means to obey and *commandment* speaks of a specific instruction regarding a place to go or a task to perform. Mom may assign chores, but the commandment to do what mom says is a message from dad.

Another aspect of dad's role is mentioned in Proverbs 4:20. The text says to attend to dad's words and incline the ear to his sayings. The terms *words* and *sayings* suggest that dad gives answers to questions that might be raised and that he serves as a counselor and adviser. "Go ask your mother" is unacceptable when children are inquiring about a matter. "Talk to the pastor and see what he thinks" is a poor substitute for godly counsel from dad. Dad is supposed to have answers and when he does not know, he must take time to find the answers.

Do these verses eliminate mom from being a source of counsel? Of course not! Should a young person ever talk to the pastor? Of course, but dad must understand his role clearly. He is the head of the home. This is more than being the one who makes final decisions in facing problems or spending money. He exercises the full leadership over the home in general and over every member of the family in particular.

Finally, we read in Proverbs 5:1, *"My son, attend unto my wisdom, and bow down thine ear to my understanding." Wisdom* and *understanding* are wonderful terms conveying discernment, understanding, discretion, and intelligence. When the text says *attend,* it means to "prick up the ears." When it says *bow down,* the meaning is to yield and surrender. Dad is to be a man who knows how to live, how to treat people, how to respond to challenges, and how to maintain spiritual perspective in trial. He is able to teach these things to his child—who when facing hard times and difficult people, needs a compassionate instructor who demonstrates a genuine walk with the Lord and a godly example, worthy of imitation.

Both Old and New Testaments give these kinds of assignments to dad. We would do well to see them as a message from the Lord. Dad's role, as seen in Scripture, is neither cultural nor archaic. The truth of Scripture is timeless truth related to God's plan for the family, as He created it and intended it. Rejecting God's Word in light of a changing culture is not progress. It is a fall from truth and it will bring severe consequences on the home and family that chooses its own way, rather than God's revealed plan.

Mom is not a second class citizen in family life. God has clearly assigned specific obligations to her. She will participate in many of the responsibilities the Lord has given to dad, but she will do so in a role supportive of his leadership. This divinely planned balance for home life and leadership provides the best opportunity for successful parenting.

Struggling Moms

You may be reading this chapter feeling great frustration as a mom who feels like what is said here may be fine for some families, but your husband is not doing the job. You may be trying to do your best, but it seems like he does not care, is too busy with work, or simply does not make family a priority. What should you do? That would certainly be a fair question and thankfully the Scripture gives us guidelines for such situations. Ephesians 5:22-23 says, *"Wives, submit yourselves unto your own husbands, as unto the Lord. For the husband is the head of the wife, even as Christ is the head of the church: and he is the savior of the body."* Notice the text tells the Christian wife to submit herself to her husband. The term *submit* speaks of ranking under another. The woman is to realize that when it comes to family order, she ranks under her husband. Sometimes a husband does not care about certain things, so the wife must go out of her way to submit herself. She can and should approach her husband to get counsel on what to do in a given situation.

For instance, a child may come to mom with a problem, which is an area that should really be addressed by dad, but dad is too busy. Mom could simply take charge and handle the matter. She would be far wiser to present the matter to her husband. He may say he does not care or he is too busy and will then hand the matter over to mom. That is fine. Mom has fulfilled her scriptural obligation and, now with dad's okay, she can minister to her child and help with the problem.

Moms put themselves and their families on dangerous spiritual ground when they think their husbands do not care and take matters into their own hands. It would be easier to just do what seems best, but God has given family order and we should honor it. One of the tendencies of wives is to take over, especially when men do not do their part. Resist that tendency and go the second mile in order to fulfill God's plan for the home. The extra effort in submitting to the husband's headship will pay off with spiritual dividends.

Single Parents

Over 90% of all single parent homes are headed by moms, so the normal family pattern laid out in the Bible cannot be experienced in those families. Many times in conferences, after I have spoken about the man's role, a lady will come up and say, "So where do I and my children stand? There is no dad in our home." These situations, of course, result most commonly from divorce, but often children have been born out of wedlock or the father has died. The cause of a particular family situation may bring trouble in other areas, but when it comes to fulfilling roles, it does not matter why mom is single.

Let's consider a few spiritual and practical helps for the single mom. Having been reared in a single parent home, I had some "baggage" growing up, but what a blessing it was to come to know Jesus Christ as my Savior shortly after graduating from high school. Sometime after my salvation I was introduced to two very important overlapping scriptural concepts, which made all the difference in the world for me as I continued to mature and eventually moved toward my own opportunity for marriage and parenthood.

Psalm 27:10 reads, *"When my father and my mother forsake me, then the LORD will take me up."* To forsake means to leave, walk away, and abandon. I was grateful for my mom, who though she never got saved until after I was in the ministry, was a faithful hard-working single parent for many years. On the other hand, I had been forsaken by my dad. Even after I got saved and made contact with him, there was no response. The Bible says that when we are forsaken the LORD will take us up. *To take up* means to receive. I accepted the message of hope and consolation—God said, if your parents abandon you, I will receive you. I cannot express the comfort and assurance that truth brought to my soul. The bitterness in my heart fell away. I had not missed anything growing up without a dad that could not be reclaimed in Christ. I did not have to bemoan my growing up years. The LORD was there for me, to teach me and equip me to be the husband to my wife that He wanted me to be and the dad to my children that I never experienced in my family.

A similar and overlapping truth is given in Psalm 68:5, which says, *"A father of the fatherless, and a judge of the widows, is God in his holy habitation."* When I accepted that truth, I thought, "There it is; I have lost nothing." What I might have had in a godly dad, I have in the personal ministry of the holy and loving God of Heaven. He will teach me, He will counsel me, and He will be there for me—never slumbering, never too busy. I do not have any regrets for having never had my dad.

So if your children are growing up the same way, these spiritual truths must be built day by day into the heart and soul of your children. Remind them of the Lord's presence, love, and faithfulness. He will never leave them nor forsake them. Look continually for opportunities to teach them these critical truths. If they will receive them and learn to lean on the Lord, they will do fine as they grow up. Yes, hard times will come for them and for mom—but God is faithful.

If you are a single mom, let me suggest some practical advice about rearing and training your children. Without the presence of a dad, you must give the care and guidance to your children, normally given by a dad. No one else can make the decisions nor solve the problems. Seek a godly man from whom you can get advice and counsel. It may be your dad, if he knows the Lord. It may be a godly brother or older man at church. It may be your pastor or some-one else in the Lord's service. You will have to make the decisions, but men and women look at things differently and respond differently to problems and pressures. The perspective and experience of a godly man may help you view matters with appropriate balance. That man or men may also be a help to your children, so they can see a living testimony for Christ in a Christian man who loves the Lord.

Be careful to maintain a strong parental relationship to your children. Single moms have a tendency to let down necessary parental barriers and become "friends" to their children instead of maintaining a strong mother role. For instance, mom's loneliness may cause her to forsake consistent bedtimes for her children. She lets them stay up because they provide company for her. They need consistent bedtimes for their training and well being. She may be lax in enforcing other standards, because she gets tired and it doesn't seem worth the effort to battle with a stubborn child.

Sometimes, because few people are available to confide in, single moms discuss problems and decisions with their children. They tell them of financial burdens and ask their advice about decisions to be made. Children are not mentally, emotionally, or spiritually prepared to enter into these adult areas of life. Maintain the difference so you will always be mom. You cannot forsake that role, even if you feel you need the emotional support that a maturing child can give. Seek advice from other godly adults in whom you can confide.

Being a single parent, especially a single mom is very tough, but it can ultimately be very rewarding. The promise of special help from the Lord can give great encouragement to carry on faithfully.

Please do not rush into a marriage, even if you are on solid scriptural ground to establish a new relationship. Often a new relationship for a single parent brings heartache to the children. The man, who a single mom thinks will meet the father need for her children, may do more to take her away from the children then to meet their needs. Believe it or not, statistically, children who grow up in a single parent home turn out with far fewer problems than children who grow up in a step family. Children in a step family often experience more loneliness and sadness, and take up the use of tobacco, alcohol, and drugs in greater numbers than young people in a single parent home. The devoted single parent tends to invest far more time and attention into their children's lives than the parent who seeks a new marriage partner. Sacrifice the necessary years to be as close to your children as possible—physically, emotionally, and spiritually.

***

When both parents are in the home it is necessary to work in close cooperation and harmony. While distinctions are made in parental roles, those roles are not carried out independently. Dads and moms must work hard to communicate with each other to find agreement in every aspect of home life. They should seek to guide their home based on biblical directives and principles. Where no scriptural injunction is clear, they should work hard to find a standard which each can heartily support. When parents are committed to the Scriptures and devoted to the physical, mental, emotional, and spiritual well being of their children, they can fulfill their God-given assignments with a happy home life and the Lord's richest blessings. The single parent has different pressures, but the single parent home can also have the rich blessings of the Lord.

9 WHAT ABOUT THE TEEN YEARS?

More often than not, at a Family Conference, I am asked if I am going to speak on teenagers and how parents can be successful in dealing with them. Unfortunately, some of the things that need to be said concerning teens come too late for many families. One thing is certain—*The better parenting we do when the children are little, the easier it will be when they get older.*

Sometimes parents pay little attention to biblical teaching when children are young, but when problems develop as the children get older, those same parents are looking hard for answers. Fortunately for some and unfortunately for others, the tree grows as it is bent. Assuming parents have done a pretty good job with little ones, there is great hope for success with them as teens.

In Proverbs 22:6 where it says, *"Train up a child in the way he should go: and when he is old, he will not depart from it,"* the term *child* refers to a child from infancy to adolescence. This suggests two things. First, training must begin early. Second, training is still going on through the adolescent years. The term *old* refers to an old person. It is not when a child is a young adult that he will not depart from what he has been trained. His training will affect him for the rest of his life. The same word *sur*, translated depart, is also found in Genesis 49:10, when the Bible says, *"The sceptre shall not 'depart' from Judah."* That makes "depart" a pretty strong word, offering parents a great deal of hope in Proverbs 22:6. As surely as the scepter shall not depart from Judah, so children (when they get old) will not depart from their training. The key is to actually train successfully and the key to successful training is to start early and to keep it going through the adolescent years. Parents must not back away from their teens and be duped by the old "generation gap" theory. These years are an important time to continue the training process.

Sometimes young people say parents "don't understand." I do not know any parents who were born as adults. The world changes, but people don't. We have all come through the teen experience. We have been there.

The adolescent years bring unique changes and challenges to the young person, so careful guidance is needed to help him succeed. As parents, we must wisely use the Word of God, our testimony for Christ, and our own life experience to help our children succeed in their lives.

Teens Need Reality in the Parent's Life

Parents need to realize that some things are more important regarding parental success when the children are younger and other things are more important when the children are older. The reason is that as children get older they are more observant and more perceptive. In other words, as they move toward maturity, they will see parents for who they really are.

Proverbs 20:7 says, *"The just man walketh in his integrity: his children are blessed after him."* Nothing is particularly mysterious about this text, nor about its fulfillment in the experience of a family. The *just man* in the Old Testament might well be understood as the saved man. As he walks in integrity, his children will see his life and pattern themselves after him. His life of integrity will be passed on to them and they will subsequently inherit the blessings of living a godly life.

Let's give some examples. When a child is four years of age, the fact that his father's church attendance is sporadic does not impact his thinking very much. When he is fourteen, it will mean much more to him. If he is a typical child, the time will come when he will not want to faithfully attend services. Opportunities to do other things on Sundays and Wednesday nights will abound. When he is told he must go to church, he will quickly remind everyone that dad does not go, so why should he? Of course at that point, parental authority may prevail, as he is required to do what he is told, not necessarily what he sees. However, the die is cast. That young person will probably avoid church as much as possible when he finally makes decisions for himself. On the other hand, the dad who is faithful will build a testimony of spiritual integrity. His son may also reach a time when he will not want to go to church whenever the doors are open, but the consistency in his dad's life will be a powerful motivation to do what is right before the Lord. This same basic scenario will be repeated in numerous areas of life. Why should we expect children to pray and have a devotional time, if parents don't? Why would we think they will care about self discipline in attitudes, words, and actions if their parents manifest little self control?

Consider a significant text from I Timothy 4:12—*"Let no man despise thy youth; but be thou an example of the believers, in word, in conversation, in charity, in spirit, in faith, in purity."* Paul wrote those words to Timothy to encourage him, because Timothy felt his ministry would not be accepted since he was still a young man. Paul told Timothy that his youth may be despised, but the genuineness of his testimony could not be denied by anyone. His message was to let the reality of his life for Christ speak out in word, conversation, charity, spirit, faith, and purity.

Timothy's feelings were not unique. Many people believe no one will pay attention to them for one reason or another. Some think they are too young, while others think they are too old. Some think they have not been saved long enough to be respected, and another thinks he is not smart enough to be respected. On it goes. The principle underneath Paul's challenge to Timothy is applicable to all and certainly to parents. Many moms and dads think their teens will reject their counsel and advice, because they are their parents. Paul would say, "Don't let your child despise you because you are his parent; let him see the reality of your Christianity in word, conversation, etc." A parent's testimony cannot be denied if it is genuine and eventually it will win the respect of the children, even if they are teens.

Teens will use parental weakness to their own advantage. Parental flaws will be the teen's justification for doing wrong. "You don't go, so why should I have to go?" Parents may have the authority to send their child where they want them to go, but the use of authority without integrity to back it up undermines respect.

Teens Need Standards for Living and Goals to Achieve

Unfortunately standards are lowering among God's people in homes, churches, and Christian schools. Living for Christ is not presented as a high and holy calling, worthy of our best. Parents must raise the standards and help children establish achievable but challenging goals.

Consider the powerful words spoken by the writer of the Proverbs to his children, as recorded for us in Proverbs 4:1-5—

"Hear, ye children, the instruction of a father, and attend to know understanding. For I give you good doctrine, forsake ye not my law. For I

was my father's son, tender and only beloved in the sight of my mother.
He taught me also, and said unto me, Let thine heart retain my words:
Keep my commandments, and live. Get wisdom, get understanding: for-
get it not; neither decline from the words of my mouth."

Here was a dad who was communicating with his children. He instructed them and taught them. He disciplined them when necessary. He challenged them to take into their hearts his words and commandments because he was telling them how to live successfully. He encouraged them to seek wisdom and understanding, and he endeavored to mentor and counsel them in those areas. He was certain of his own convictions and standards, so he exhorted his children to never decline (put away or walk away) from the words of his mouth. He was raising standards and inspiring his children toward full surrender.

Teenagers need to have solid, biblically-based convictions by which to live. They need parents who will care enough and be prepared enough to instruct them regarding standards that are appropriate for godly people. This is important—when times of testing come, standards based on the Word of God must never be lowered. If parents compromise every time a teenager pushes the boundaries and questions the rules, soon the home will have no standards, control, or discipline. Beyond that, however, standards and rules of conduct must be supported by giving teens a framework for living.

Assuming the teen has professed to receive Christ as his Savior, he needs kind and encouraging reminders that *we are Christians, we believe the Bible,* and *we live by the Bible.* In a day when the people of the world are not afraid to be different from everyone else for the sake of their cause, Christian young people need to have set before them the fact that we are called to serve in the greatest cause on this earth.

One of the problems among Christians today is that we are trying to make Christianity easy. Praise the Lord, becoming a Christian is easy because the Savior paid the price with His shed blood; however, it is no easy task to live as a Christian. In trying to make Christian living easy and convenient, we have lowered the standards. How we act, what we do, or how we dress does not matter. Does this prevailing attitude match the scriptural challenge to live for Christ?

Consider the words of our Lord in Mark 8:34-35—"*...Whosoever will come after me, let him deny himself, and take up his cross, and follow me. For whosoever will save his life shall lose it; but whosoever shall lose his life for my sake and the gospel's, shall save it.*" Teens need to know that the cause of Christ is so great that it demands their all. They should act sharp, dress sharp, have high standards, and be willing to stand alone for the Lord of Lords. They should be challenged to put their all on the altar and do great things for Christ. Unsaved people should be warmly received in the Christian setting no matter how they appear, but Christians should be taught to give their best to the Lord. Too many parents are begging their children to do right. Words like "I don't care how you dress as long as you go" are tragic. The work of Christ is the greatest work that exists and it should not be carried on in the context of apathy, complacency, and mediocrity. Let's raise the standards for our children, not lower them.

Parents will have problems creating highly motivated servants of God if they are not fully surrendered themselves. On the other hand, if parents have a genuine testimony, are zealous for Christ, and are highly motivated to live for Him, a good chance exists that their children will catch the vision.

Parents must help teens establish character goals and service goals in their Christian life. Encourage them to identify with God's servants whose lives and testimonies are recorded in Scripture. Who could be a better example for a girl than Esther, who was willing to surrender everything for the cause of God's people? What of the qualities found in Ruth, Hannah, Lydia, or Priscilla? Who could be held in higher esteem for a boy than Daniel, who willingly faced the den of lions? But then there is also Joshua, Joseph, Stephen, and Paul.

Parents can provide more help and motivation by giving their teenagers service opportunities. Mission trips, working in VBS, a bus route, Junior Church, working at a Christian camp, and being involved in other ministries can help stir a burden for souls. The bottom line is that young people must be given a reason to live that transcends position, popularity, and prosperity. They need a cause with which to identify. They need something worthwhile into which they can invest their lives in sacrificial devotion. Could there be any cause greater than the work of God? They might represent Him in preaching or teaching. They might serve Him as a lawyer, police officer, business executive, carpenter, or plumber—but to serve Him is their calling. Parents must encourage them to give all.

I have often illustrated devotion to Christ with the experience of a young man who fell in love. He did not want to go to church. He did not even want to dress properly, comb his hair, or polish his shoes. His parents were very frustrated. One Sunday he came down from his bedroom ready for Sunday School. He looked good, smelled good, and was ready to go 15 minutes ahead of time. His parents could not figure out what happened until they got to church. The young man got out of the car and headed for his class. There his parents saw a young lady waiting for their son. What made the young man give his best was quite easy to figure out. He was in love.

Young people today often resist going to church and doing things right. They tell us all is well spiritually. This I will guarantee you—when that teen comes to the point in his life when he truly loves the Savior, dad and mom will never have another struggle getting him to do the right thing for the Lord. Let them see their parent's love for Christ and that same love may take hold of their heart.

Teens Need Balanced and Appropriate Discipline

As a young person reaches the teen years, the ability to discipline effectively becomes a greater challenge. The use of the rod is no longer appropriate, and other options are limited. If discipline has been effective in early years, respect for mom and dad should be established. This is important because our authority is primarily spiritual, based on the fact that God has entrusted our children to us. By the teen years much of the foolishness (Proverbs 22:15) should be out of the child's heart, and the greater challenge, to build wisdom (Proverbs 29:15) into the heart, becomes primary.

If serious conflict is in the home, it is absolutely essential that parents avoid any physical confrontation with their teen. If early training has been successful, this will not even be an issue, but we must emphasize it. On occasion I hear of a dad blocking the door to keep his son from going out or putting his son up against the wall to prove dad is still stronger. This kind of authoritarian behavior is way out of bounds.

So what does a parent do? It is important that love is always affirmed to a young person. *"You are not allowed to go, but I love you"* or *"You are going and by the way, I love you"* are the kinds of phrases that can help. Of course, teens often want to measure right and wrong by what others are doing. They frequently give a list of everyone else who is allowed to go to justify their request. Parents must answer firmly, but lovingly. Hopefully, parents will have good spiritual and practical reasons why a particular event is not the place for their child to be. If a spiritual foundation is in the teen's heart, he may complain, but underneath will have to acknowledge the correct decision by his parents.

Teens need to know that their home is not being unduly influenced by other families. The goal of their home is to set an example of godliness, not simply follow the crowd. The teen should be encouraged to take on that role in his own personal life and testimony. The question is not "how many others are doing it?" The question is "will it honor the Lord?" It is also important for the parent to respond, not react, when an issue needs to be discussed. Raising of the voice, belittling the teen, or calling his salvation into question is not the best way to handle a difficult situation. The teen needs to see that his parents have a quiet resolve about the issue and that it is not up for debate.

When I came to know the Lord, one of the things to go from my life was attendance at the movie theater. I knew it was no place for me as a Christian. These days more and more Christians seem to be going, and it is not as if movies have gotten any better in the last 40 years. There is more sensuality, violence, and vulgarity then ever. In any event, it would not be unlikely today for a Christian young person to come home and ask permission to go to a movie. The justification for asking might be that it is a "great" movie, with incredible virtual technology and, besides, all the teens in the class are going. How does a parent respond? Now if the parent allows the worst of today's videos to be watched at home, it will be pretty tough to take a stand. Assuming the best of standards for the home, however, dad can respond by reminding the teen that the family has a consistent standard which does not allow for such movies. As suggested earlier, raising the voice or calling the spiritual life of the teen into question should not happen. This is a time for quiet resolve and the reminder that our home does not follow the crowd, we put Christ first.

A wise parental tactic is to require requests be made well in advance, so the parents have time to get all appropriate details about an event. Is it appropriate for a Christian? Where will it be? When does it start? When does it end? Who will be in charge? Early requests also give parents time to communicate with each other so the decision can be made in harmony. Often a young person will come with the plea that they have to have an answer immediately. In our home that always made it easy. If the children had to know immediately, the answer was automatically no.

In all of these kinds of circumstances it is fair and reasonable for the teens to have a clear explanation of what is expected of them, and then parents must consistently follow through. Dads and moms sometimes get caught in situations they had not expected, so they change the rules in the middle of the game. This kind of experience only creates bitterness in a young person. When a teen thinks he has met all of the qualifications for doing certain things or going certain places and then is told no, real tension is created. Parents sometimes defend their position by saying they changed their mind or created new rules.

I am reminded of a situation where a teenage boy was planning to go to a church youth outing. He fulfilled all the normal obligations. He had all the details of who, what, where, and when. When the time for the event came, his parents announced that he could not go. When he asked why, he was told his parents had changed their mind and no other explanation was given. He was angry and bitter. Behind the scene was information the parents had received that a certain young lady was going to the event because she hoped to attract their son. The boy knew nothing of it and was deprived of the opportunity to go because his parents reacted to a rumor. Their failure to open up the matter and discuss it with their son only created anger in him, because his parents changed the rules. The desire of the girl brought punishment to an innocent boy. Teens need to know what is expected of them. When they do their part, they should be sure parents will do their part.

If a teen acts in such a way that discipline is required, parents must exercise great wisdom. While we do not want a matter to linger, it may be wise to take some time to consider carefully what the discipline will be. Proverbs 14:17 says, *"He that is soon angry dealeth foolishly..."* and Proverbs 14:29b says, *"He that is hasty of spirit exalteth folly."* Parents can tell the teen that discipline is coming, but they will discuss it and make a decision after they have thought about the matter. Why can this be helpful? Parents will legitimately have time to think, talk and, hopefully, come to agreement on the matter. This is important because teens, as much as we love them, can be masters at dividing and conquering. We also want to avoid the folly that can accompany hastiness. It will also give the young person time to think about his actions and attitudes. The attitude he has when the time comes to discuss the matter may have bearing on the ultimate response of dad and mom.

The beauty of using the rod when the child is young is the fact that the discipline is over quickly and the matter can be put behind everyone. When a teen is disciplined, handling a matter effectively and efficiently is much tougher. If parents overreact and discipline too harshly, they may run out of options when and if disobedience and disrespect continues.

Sometimes the best initial response to a problem is a serious one-on-one discussion and appropriate rebuke. This first step of discipline and all discipline that might follow is founded on the fact that parents have spiritual authority over their children and that authority has been given by God. A dad and mom should never downplay this authority and, in fact, should make the most of it.

Disobeying parents should be understood as disobeying God. A significant statement about authority is found in I Samuel 8:7. The people of Israel demanded a king and Samuel was deeply hurt by their demand. The Lord encouraged him by saying, *"...they have not rejected thee, but they have rejected me, that I should not reign over them."* Children must be taught and teens must be reminded that disobedience and willfulness on their part is not only a rejection of their parents, but disobedience toward the Lord. They must know that they are never beyond the bounds of God's sight and will always ultimately be answerable to Him. Appealing to a teen from a spiritual perspective is a very important disciplinary tool. One of the most important truths we will ever teach our children is accountability to the Lord. Parents need to teach this lesson early and often.

When actual disciplinary action is necessary, we have some options. One might be to require extra work and chores. Another would be to take away privileges. I would offer a couple of cautions here. Unless the problem involves church activities, do not refuse your teen the privilege of going to church-sponsored programs as part of their punishment. I know of times when teens appeared to make real spiritual progress under the church youth program. Then when they did something wrong at home, their punishment was to keep them home from church. We want them to be under good spiritual teaching as often as possible. Also I would suggest that unless the matter is very serious, we should not use refusal to attend a special event as a vehicle for punishment. I can think of times from the past when a young person had been planning for a long time to attend summer camp or had been hoping to attend a church youth banquet. Unfortunately, these rare and special events were taken away from the teen in punishment for a minor issue of disobedience. The problem just happened to occur close to the time for those events. The old adage that the punishment should fit the crime is appropriate for teen discipline, but in those instances, was forgotten. The discipline only created unnecessary resentment. Keep disciplinary procedures in the context of normal activities.

Also, if possible, try to make sure punishment for your teen does not affect too many other people. I have seen young people on a sports team be kept home from a game as punishment. As a result, many suffered. Involvement on a team requires commitment. Teen should be encouraged to keep their commitments. Punish in other areas.

You might be wondering what you can do if so many areas are off limits. You can use such things as driving privileges, TV & video privileges, computer privileges, and phone privileges to name a few. You can assign projects—whether it is work, writing, or reading. Look for things that have impact on your child. He may love it if you give him a reading assignment, but he may suffer a bit more if he is not allowed to drive for a time. Be wise in how you handle these things. I have seen some parents use such harsh discipline that nothing was left to do in the future. In response to such harshness, rebellious teens persist in their disobedience feeling like nothing else could be done to them.

What if the teen seems to be incorrigible? I have had parents call me and say they have tried everything, but their child is unreachable. DO NOT, I repeat, DO NOT threaten to send your child away. This seems like the new trend among Christian families and it breaks my heart. I have seen it in the family life of men in the ministry, and it is being repeated in many Christian homes. Men in the ministry have done it because their child has been an embarrassment to them. They have thought that if they got their child off the scene it might preserve their own opportunity to serve in a church. The Lord clearly put proper family relationships as prerequisite for ministry. If the family is not right, then the opportunity to minister is forfeited. The Scriptures in I Timothy 3 and Titus 1 do not say children must be perfect, but they cannot be out and out rebels.

The family was ordained by God before human government or the church. What is of prime importance to Him should be of prime importance to us. The message to our children, however, must be that God gave them to us and, though they may choose to run away from home, they will never be told to leave nor will they ever be sent away. Obviously, certain standards should be held in the home and they should never be lowered. The teen will be expected to conform. Discipline will be at whatever level is necessary to bring about conformity, but, when all is said and done, *home is home.*

Whether one is in the ministry or not, the child is ours and, next to our marriage, holds the highest priority among human relationships. If we send our children away, we send at least two messages. The first is to the child that we sent away. We let him know that he has become too much trouble for us, so we are hoping someone else will do for him what we have been unable to accomplish. The second message is to the other children in the family. It says, "You better do right, because if you don't, you will be sent away, too." No, we should not want to pass these messages on to our children. Difficult times that may cause parents to consider such extraordinary measures should instead create spiritual determination in us that says, "God gave this child to us and we will do everything within our power to win him to the Lord and to us."

If parents ever face such a situation, they may need to seek help from a pastor or godly friend, but they must also consider when rebellion began and what contributed to it. Time after time in counseling situations, it has proved valuable to find out what happened, when it happened, and who was involved when the pattern of open rebellion began. Find out the source of the difficulty and you find the best chance to get things resolved.

Teens Need Compassionate Understanding

Psalm 103:13-14 reads, *"Like as a father pitieth his children, so the LORD pitieth them that fear him. For he knoweth our frame; he remembereth that we are dust."*

What a great text! Every honest Christian will tell how grateful he is for the pity of the Lord. The Hebrew term translated *pity* means compassionate understanding. The text tells us the Lord knows our frame and remembers that we are dust. The God of infinite power and majesty looks at us and remembers continually that we were molded from the dust of the ground. We are very frail and feeble creatures. God understands.

Amazing to me is that the Scriptures liken the pity of God to the pity of a father toward his children. Fathers are supposed to have compassionate understanding of their children. Why is this necessary? Because all children, and especially teens, struggle to handle the responsibilities and challenges of life. They need help in facing their battles and their fears. Consider some of those battles and fears with me.

The beginning of adolescence is marked by puberty. This is that stage of maturity when the young person becomes capable of sexual reproduction, a time of physical change and development. It is also a time when a typical teen may receive a lot of information from his friends and almost no information from his parents. New fears, curiosity, and desires to accompany those dramatic physical changes may awaken.

Parents need to sharpen their communication skills and have the lines of communication open to help their child through this new level of life. It is not a time to simply give them a book to read or a video to watch. By the way, it is also not a time for the teen Sunday School class or the Youth Group to start a series on the topic. These issues are very personal and development in one child may be far ahead or far behind another young person. This is a time for parents to be keenly aware of where their child is in development and understanding, so they can be of help to their teenager. It might be good for dad and mom to read a book or two in order to prepare for some tough, but important conversations. This is not a time to pull away from our teens; it is a time when they need our understanding and counsel.

Another area that teens face which can stir fears in them is the thought of the future. They wonder if they can make it through high school. Some are terrified at the thought of college. Many have no desire to leave home, have no idea what to choose for a major area of study, and have no firm plans for what they want to do as a vocation. To add to those personal internal challenges is a changing culture that may threaten their feelings of security and a violent world, plagued today by war and terrorism. How desperately they need parents who will talk with them, counsel them, and pray with them in preparation for the day they will step out on their own.

Friendships are usually very important to teens. Choosing and maintaining friendships can be a battleground for young people. Peer pressure from without and a seeming natural desire for acceptance within can make things pretty tough when selecting close acquaintances. The Bible is clear enough when it says in Proverbs 13:20, *"He that walketh with wise men shall be wise: but a companion of fools shall be destroyed."* And Proverbs 1:10 states, *"My son, if sinners entice thee, consent thou not."*

In the day-to-day experience of going to school and church, making and maintaining good friendships while avoiding bad ones is not as easy as it sounds. One way to help is to encourage the establishment of criteria for friendships before a crisis arises. Ask a 10 year old to make a list of the qualities he desires in a friend and you may get a good foundation on which to build. Ask a 15 year old and the list may lack much in the way of conviction.

Here are a few suggestions about friendship. An unsaved "friend" is a mission field. If I do not have an established testimony before him and if I am not constantly looking for ways to tell him about Christ, the friendship has no place in my life. If I am not seeking to win him to Christ, he will take me into sin.

If I have a friend who is saved or who claims to be, I need to consider the purpose and value of the friendship. Proverbs 27:17 tells me, *"Iron sharpeneth iron; so a man sharpeneth the countenance of his friend."* It is good to have friends. We do not function best living in isolation. Part of the purpose of friendship, however, is to sharpen the countenance of one another. One conceives an idea but interaction with his friend brings evaluation, criticism, perfection, or rejection of the initial thought. Perhaps one entertains the thought of sin, but his friend holds him accountable and encourages him to do right. One is discouraged, but his friend upholds him with kindness and consolation. Friends sharpen one another. We need to be sharp for Christ. Only the right kind of friends can help us. We need to help our teens understand that they cannot be good friends to others until they are willing to stand alone for Christ. When they have firmly established convictions, they can help sharpen the countenance of their friends and they will tend to pick friends who can do the same for them.

Another area where teens need help is handling the pressures of participation and competition in academics, athletics, and fine arts. Abilities and interests in these areas vary greatly among all young people and even within the same family. In our walk with the Lord, we find comfort when we realize He loves us for who we are and is no respecter of persons. He wants us to do our best with the talents we have been given, and we are never measured through comparison with someone else. We must help our young people find balance in handling success and failure. The fact remains that recognition, popularity, and favor with many people are often related to success in academics, fine arts, and athletics. The truth is that some will succeed with very little effort, some will succeed with a great deal of effort, and some will not succeed regardless of their effort.

For parents to maintain spiritual perspective responding to these differences and helping their children do the same can be very tough. We must continually focus on how the Lord looks at these issues. We must give honor to whom honor is due. Nothing is wrong with having a class valedictorian, a single winner in fine arts competition, or a most valuable player on an athletic team. Let us give honor to whom honor is due. Personal qualities and personal effort, however, can also be recognized such as most improved, diligence, and sportsmanship.

Parents must make every effort to help their children understand there is a place for the Corruptible Crown, but it will mean little if it is not accompanied by the Incorruptible Crown (I Corinthians 9:24-27). And if for some reason one must be chosen over the other, let it be the Incorruptible Crown and a clear testimony for Christ. The exhortation to young people must always be that they do their best for the Lord. Nothing is of greater importance. If teens can add to doing their best for the Lord a gracious attitude whether winning or losing, they will be far ahead of many of their peers.

Also in the teen years, temptation to sin takes on new dimensions. A number of factors contribute to this expanding realm of moral and spiritual danger. Teens typically have more time on their own than younger children. Many activities take them out of the house and into the sphere of temptation. After-school activities, youth activities, part-time jobs, or outings with other young people sometimes have lax adult supervision. These experiences not only put young people on their own, but often present new potential acquaintances who may not be known or approved by dad and mom. Too often the time comes when someone offers a young person that first experience with tobacco, alcohol, or drugs. Physical development and newly awakened interests in the opposite sex present moral challenges unknown to younger children.

Proper parental response to this new range of temptation will not always be appreciated by teens—but this is a critical time for parents to know where teens are, with whom they are spending time, and what time they will be home. This is a time for increased, not decreased, accountability. If for some reason plans change in the middle of an outing, parents should be immediately notified. If the teen is going to be a late, a phone call is appropriate.

Much of parenting is providing protection for children. The world is wicked, the flesh is weak, and the Devil is pernicious. Parents must seek to guard their children from falling into sinful error that may tarnish their testimony and ruin their lives. Teens often feel that requiring accountability reflects a lack of trust from parents. Teens need to be taught that their challenge is to earn trust by acting responsibly, which will include very open communication with their parents. As the teens demonstrate maturing actions and attitudes, they should be granted more liberty to be on their own and make more of their own decisions.

Teens Need Parents to Stay Involved in Their Lives and Activities

Deuteronomy 6:6-7 says, *"And these words, which I command thee this day, shall be in thine heart: And thou shalt teach them diligently unto thy children, and shalt talk of them when thou sittest in thine house, and when thou walkest by the way, and when thou liest down, and when thou risest up."*

Here is a text that demands personal involvement with our children. It reminds us that "quality time" is not enough—we must have "quantity time" with our children. Backing away from our teens and their activities is too easy and, therefore, we miss the opportunities to fulfill the challenge of these verses.

When children are younger, parents are often the only means of transportation to activities. They are often involved in events as chaperones or spectators. When teens have activities, they may drive themselves or get a ride with someone else. That opens the door for parents to be involved in other affairs or pursue their own interests during their free time. Children want a measure of independence as they get older, but parents must not jump ship on their responsibilities. Parents find out that bypassing an event is easy because a teen does not ask the parent to go and the parent does not really want to go anyway. My encouragement to parents is to attend activities as much as possible when your child is involved.

Is there a parent-teacher meeting at school? I would tell parents to go to meet the teacher and get an evaluation of the child's attitudes, actions, and work habits. Is there an athletic event or special program? I would encourage attendance if in any way possible. Does the teen have a part-time job? I suggest the parent meet the boss and show interest in the child's endeavors. Are there friends the teen talks about whom the parents have never met? I recommend having a get-together and invite the friends so the parents can get to know them.

Along with involvement in activities and friends, parents should go out of the way to make personal time with each of their children. I wish I had done more of it, but some of my most treasured memories with my children are the one-on-one experiences of discussing a problem or just discussing life—times when we were together without a schedule hanging over our heads. They were not times of pressure or tension. They were times when we could open our hearts and hear from each other. They were times when I could share the testimony of things I learned in my walk with Christ, not wielding my parental authority, but gently encouraging a deeper trust in the Lord. When Moses talked of teaching our children when sitting in the house, walking by the way, lying down, or rising up, he was not talking about formal times or times of discipline. He was encouraging personal, intimate, tender times when a child could hear from a loving parent. Do you ever have those times?

Teens Need to be Assured of Forgiveness and Unconditional Love

Forgiveness is a wonderful aspect of God's gracious dealings with us as sinners. Think of the ways the Lord illustrates the completeness and finality of His actions in lovingly forgiving us. In Psalm 103:12 He puts it this way—*"As far as the east is from the west, so far hath he removed our transgressions from us."* In Micah 7:19 we read, *"He will turn again, he will have compassion upon us;... and thou wilt cast all their sins into the depths of the sea."* A chorus we sing says, *"...buried in the deepest sea, yes that's good enough for me..."*

Then in rehearsing the blessings of the New Covenant, Jeremiah records the words of the Lord in Jeremiah 31:34 when He said, *"...for I will forgive their iniquity, and I will remember their sin no more."* The term *remember* means to mark so as to recognize or to mention. The omnipotent God will always remember (be cognizant of) all things. Praise Him however, He will not mark us with them or mention them once we have been forgiven. He will not bring them up again or hold them against us.

Teenagers will need to be forgiven many times. In the midst of growing, learning, and maturing, they will sin and fail on numerous occasions. Parents hope that teens will repent, face their sin, and forsake it. When teens humble themselves and seek forgiveness, they need parents to bury those sins in the deepest sea. Forgiveness should bring a fresh start. Continual reminders of failure will only bring discouragement. If the sin has not been acknowledged and dealt with or if it continues, then it must be brought up again—but once confessed and forsaken it must not be mentioned anymore.

Associated with the idea of forgiveness in the teens is the need for unconditional love. Unconditional love never conveys approval of wrong-doing. It does communicate assurance that love will never stop and nothing can separate the teen from the love of a parent. "I love you" are wonderful words that are often not spoken enough between teens and their folks. Let parental love never be called into question. To even talk about unconditional love suggests that things might be done that could affect the love of one person for another. It suggests that there might be certain standards that must be maintained for love to continue. An atmosphere where the love of one person for another could be put at risk is totally unacceptable.

The story of the prodigal son in Luke 15 is a great example for us. To be *prodigal* is to be reckless, wasteful, and extravagant. The younger of the two sons cared little for his father. He had no respect for the things that were important to his dad. He had no appreciation for how his father had worked to obtain his success. There was little regard for the work that would need to be done if this wasteful son left home and family. He had little concern for his brother and the affect his reckless life might have on his brother. With those rebellious attitudes, he approached his father and said he wanted the portion of goods that fell to him. How arrogant. Nothing was rightfully his while his father lived and he did not even ask; he simply stated what he wanted. The father broke up his estate and within a few days the son deserted his home to travel to a far country. There he wasted all his inherited wealth. When he finally came home, a broken young man, he found the open and loving arms of his dad. He deserved nothing, but he could not escape the love of his father.

Children can break the hearts of their parents through thoughtless words, attitudes, and actions. They can reject what is best and choose a wayward path.

In the midst of it all, they must know they are still loved. True love can bring discipline and disapproval, but genuine love will never end. This is the love the Lord has for us as recorded in Romans 8:35-39. This is the love we must demonstrate to our children as long as we live.

Teens Need Special Guidance in Developing Relationships

One of the most challenging times in dealing with our teens is when they begin to show interest in the opposite sex. Let's face the fact that such interest is normal and should not be viewed as sinful. At the same time, teens need special guidance, lots of communication with parents, and appropriate parental protection to walk through these years in purity and wholesomeness. Unfortunately concern over these matters has turned to a discussion of "dating or courting". In some instances the advocates of courting have written up a whole set of guidelines about the role of the girl, the role of the boy, the role of the girl's father, etc. Often the guidelines create totally artificial settings for developing relationships and many times fall short of being based on scriptural grounds.

The first matter that needs to be faced by parents is their obligation to oversee their children's lives. Parents are responsible for where children go, who they are with, and what they do. They are to protect their children from harm and danger. They must do everything possible to help their children move toward the day when they will select a mate for life and establish a Christian home.

The Bible gives many clear teachings that can be legitimately applied to the teen life and experience. These teachings should be used to help parents set up guidelines for their children. The teachings are the same for all, while individual parents have the obligation to decide the specifics of how the Scripture will be applied in their family. A few are listed for consideration.

> *"But put ye on the Lord Jesus Christ, and make not provision for the flesh, to fulfill the lusts thereof." Romans 13:14*

Every person has the flesh, even the sweetest Christian girl. Our challenge is to not make provision for it. That means we do not put ourselves or our children in situations where the desires of the flesh can easily take someone into sin. The most spiritual of Christian young people can fall if they are allowed private time together without proper oversight and accountability. Each set of parents must face this text and set up their standards accordingly.

> *"Whether therefore ye eat, or drink, or whatsoever ye do, do all to the glory of God." I Corinthians 10:31*

This challenge is one we teach our children, but we also use it as a guide in our determination of what teens can do and where they can go. Of course, if we are going to use it to guide them, we better use it to guide ourselves.

How might the following apply?

> *"Watch and pray, that ye enter not into temptation: the spirit indeed is willing, but the flesh is weak." Matthew 26:41*

> *"For this is the will of God, even your sanctification, that ye should abstain from fornication: That every one of you should know how to possess his vessel in sanctification and honor." I Thessalonians 4:3-4*

> *"My son, if sinners entice thee, consent thou not." Proverbs 1:10*

> *"Be not deceived, evil communications corrupt good manners." I Corinthians 15:33*

> *"I beseech you therefore, brethren, by the mercies of God, that ye present your bodies a living sacrifice, holy, acceptable unto God, which is your reasonable service. And be not conformed to this world: but be ye transformed by the renewing of your mind, that ye may prove what is that good, and acceptable, and perfect, will of God." Romans 12:1-2*

With these and other Bible truths and warnings, parents must set the guidelines for their children. Getting wise counsel will help. The pastor can give aid. Older folks who have successfully reared their children can be of invaluable assistance. When all is said and done, however, parents must take responsibility for their children. They must not yield to what other parents do; they must not give in to the pressures created by their own children; they must not simply do what the church says to do. Dad and mom, face the fact that God gave this child to you. Decisions must be made carefully, prayerfully, and with parental agreement. They must be implemented lovingly and firmly. It is no easy task to walk children through the teen years—but there are no other acceptable options for success.

One other thought should be added. Please do not get caught in the trap of assuming that all will be well because you send your child to a Christian school or even a Christian college, where you assume they will meet the finest of Christian young people. Maybe they will and maybe they will not. Many couples have met in the strict setting of the Christian college where standards were held high and relationships were built in wonderful surroundings. Campus life can be wonderful, but it is artificial in some ways. Do not yield your responsibility as a parent to the school or college administration. You are the parent whether your child is in a college dorm or in your own home. Stay actively involved and set the standard you want for your child in meeting someone and developing that relationship that may have bearing on him and the rest of your family for years to come. It will help if you set up standards before the pressure of the teen years begin to mount. It will also help if you can win your child to accept godly standards for developing a relationship before they ever take up interest in a particular person.

"Abstain from all appearance of evil." I Thessalonians 5:22

There may be situations that are not as bad as they may appear, but we cannot let our children participate in that which even has the appearance of evil.

10 ANSWERS TO COMMONLY ASKED QUESTIONS

1. How is it possible in a family with 4 children, for 3 of them to grow up and serve the Lord while one of them goes the way of the world?

The answer is not as difficult as it might seem at first. Every child is different in personality, intellect, and interests. While parents must have the same godly standards for all their children, they will have to be aware of the uniqueness of each child, being sensitive to particular needs and problems. Some studies have shown the differences that develop in children according to their place in the family. A first child seems to have certain tendencies; a second child has other tendencies. Parents must work hard to understand each child and deal with him appropriately. The compliant child may seem easier to handle, but may develop quiet inner rebellion which will show up in later years. The more active child may resist submission to authority and, if not brought to respect authority early in life, may have a very troublesome teen experience. Set clear spiritual and character goals for all your children. Realize that achieving them for some will be much tougher than for others, but achieving them (at least to a large degree) is a must for each child.

2. What if my mate and I do not agree on certain parenting practices?

This is not an unusual situation because parents often treat their children by reacting to the way they were brought up or reacting to their mate's approach. Some folks feel their own parents were too strict, so they want to be easy. Or one parent may feel the other parent is too soft, so he/she wants to be a little tougher. I would encourage you to go back to the chapter on the parent's different roles as a starting point. Reading that chapter again may help. Next, keep in mind that your goal should be to carry out parenting practices as closely as possible to the instructions given in Scripture. Find Scripture to address as many situations as possible. Talk together about your differences and try to come to agreement on those areas not directly addressed in Scripture. Finally, seek counsel from your pastor or an older couple who have raised God-honoring children. Their perspective might help. One thing is critical—you must not allow your children see that you are divided.

3. What if using the rod does not seem to work on a particular child?

The proper use of the rod will accomplish what God says it will accomplish. According to Proverbs 22:15, the rod will drive foolishness from the heart of the child. You may not see the immediate results you want and may be tempted to try another approach. Stay with God's way. Be steady and consistent. In due time, you will see the results God has promised. Children are different from each other and some will be tougher than others to win over, but God knew about all children when He gave us instructions on rearing them. He knew your little one would come along someday. Make sure you are disciplining in harmony with the Scripture. Yelling and displays of temper have no place. Make sure the time of discipline is a tender time with spiritual emphasis. Then trust the Lord. Remember, it is not what your little one is at age 5 that makes the difference. What he is at 25 will be more revealing of your success.

4. How do we implement change if we have not been disciplining properly?

It may be wise to sit down with your children to explain that your discipline has not been carried out the way the Lord wants it. Apologize and tell your children that from now on you are going to follow Scripture, because God is all wise and His way is best. Also show them the Scripture in Proverbs 13:24 that says the parent who loves his child will chasten him betimes (early). Then take time to explain to your children exactly what you are planning to do. Tell them how you will give instructions from now on and what you will expect in the way of obedience. Tell them what circumstances may require the use of the rod and exactly what will happen when that occurs. Please be sure to give these explanations in a non-crisis time, not when you are ready to discipline. Answer any questions your children may have, so you are sure they understand what you expect from them. The first time a problem arises you may want to remind them of the new way of disciplining them. Give them a warning with the sure promise that if the problem occurs again, they will be disciplined.

5. Should mom discipline or wait until dad gets home so he can deal with the problems?

Yes, mom should discipline. It is not fair to the child to spend the day fretting over dad's return from work. It is also not fair to dad to walk in from work and immediately have to confront a discipline problem. One of the benefits of disciplining God's way is that the matter is settled quickly. Everyone gets a fresh start once a problem is cared for. If a child is in continual trouble all day, mom may become very frustrated. At such times, it would be appropriate to let dad, as the head of the home, take over and resolve the matter when he comes in.

6. I have heard that in discipline we should get our child to "weep repentantly." What if my child does not?

Quiet, repentant weeping is a good sign that the discipline has brought true repentance and sorrow for wrong-doing. However, holding out for such a response every time we discipline is not wise. One reason is that some have a tendency to paddle a child into submission. This approach could easily turn to an abusive situation, if a child has a streak of stubbornness. Proper consistent discipline will be successful over time. Also, some children can be good actors. If a child knows mom and dad are expecting them to weep repentantly, they can easily give that appearance.

7. Should we make our children apologize when they do wrong?

Children should be taught that a heart-felt apology is proper in making amends for wrong doing. I would be careful about making them say words like "I am sorry" when they are not sorry. If you are going to make them apologize, require them to say words like "I was wrong. Will you forgive me?" They may not feel sorry and making them lie holds no value. They should acknowledge wrong doing and should seek appropriate forgiveness.

8. My teenager was always good and responsive at home. All of a sudden he/she has gone the wrong way. What do we do?

It would be seldom that teens or anyone else would "all of a sudden" change. I often hear the phrase "He just snapped." If he snapped, he snapped on the outside, but things have been wrong on the inside for a long time. Look back and see if at a particular time things began to move in the wrong direction and consider what circumstances may have brought on the beginnings of change. Did the teen change schools or move? Did the teen have a problem with a friend, a teacher, or a family member? What happened? Was there a struggle with one of the parents? Was there something the child really wanted to do and was refused, or a place he wanted to go and you said no? Time after time these situations occur. Time after time something happened that started a young person down a path of discouragement, fear, or anger. If you can pinpoint what happened and who was involved, you may be on your way to rescuing your teen from a lot more heartache.

The next challenge is to get the teen to talk about it. That can be a battle in itself. Keep this in mind—when asked what is wrong, his first response may be "I don't know," but the Bible says in Proverbs 14:10, *"The heart knoweth his own bitterness."* Your teen knows what is wrong. You need to get him to open up to you or someone else he will trust. When all is said and done, you will find out that he responded improperly to some circumstance in his life. Instead of turning to the Lord, he reacted in the flesh.

9. My child is very willful and resistant to authority. How can I succeed with him?

You may have considered what the Bible says about training and discipline, but feel like your child is a unique case. I want to remind you that when the Holy Spirit authored the Scriptures, He was fully aware that your child would come along some day. It can be frustrating when some children are very compliant and others stand up to defy you. Children are not all the same in personality, intelligence, or temperament.

The challenge for the parent is to take the little one wherever he is or whatever he is like and move him toward the kind of person he ought to be. That means some are going to take a lot more work than others. Steadiness and consistency are the keys to success. Of course, the temperament and personality of some children will make the parenting experience much more difficult physically and emotionally. Stay steady, consistent, and unbending with your discipline and training. It will pay off. We will reap if we don't faint. Too many parents get weary and give in or give up. Make sure to go out of your way to reward good behavior. Steadfast standards, loving discipline, positive reinforcement along with day-in-and-day-out consistency will eventually win over the willful child.

10. I know a home where everything seemed right, but some of the children chose a worldly life. What hope do we have for our children?

Your hope is in steadfast adherence to the Word of God in training and discipline of your children, protecting your children from ungodly influences, and living a Christ-honoring testimony before them. It can be discouraging when we see children from good Christian homes go astray. The simple truth is, however, we do not know what went on in that home. We do not know the patterns of discipline, the examples set by parents, or the degree of bad influences from others. The bottom line is that we must not judge the teachings of the Scriptures as inadequate for parenting, because they did not seem to work for certain families. Believe the Bible. God knows the way of truth. Trust Him.

11. *The latest theories on discipline teach that we should ignore our children's displays of temper or disobedience and simply try to redirect them to better activities. Aren't these approaches better than continual confrontation with our children?*

The Bible teaches control and train rather than ignore and redirect. Ignoring and redirecting gives full control to the willful child. He will be happy only when the parent comes up with some activity that will make him happy. What will it take to make him happy in his teen years and beyond? The child's will must be brought into submission to his parents, who are the God-given authority in his life. Parents are then to train the child how to live—serving God and respecting others. Controlling and training will create some unhappiness for the little one, but will produce a lifetime of joy in serving the Lord and living responsibly.

11 READY FOR CHANGE

Is It Too Late?

One of the first questions that may be on your mind after reading this book is simply to wonder if it is too late for your family or for a particular one of your children. That is a fair question that deserves honest consideration.

Scripture gives serious warnings about rearing children. As seen earlier, Proverbs 19:18 says, *"Chasten thy son while there is hope."* As we pointed out, such a statement conveys urgency. If you must do something while there is hope, the implication is that the time may come when there is no hope.

Consider the principle of sowing and reaping, wherein the Lord teaches us that what we sow, we must reap (Galatians 6:7). Today each of us is reaping what we have sown in the past and we will no doubt continue to reap for time to come. We reap as we have sown, be it good or bad. If things have not been done well in the past, our challenge is to start sowing now in a way that fully honors the Lord and His Word, so we can reap His blessings in the future. By God's grace, it is never too late to start doing right and to hope for change and ultimate success.

Face honestly, however, that your child has been developing patterns of behavior that may be very difficult to change. He may be willful and disrespectful and I can assure you he is not anxious for change in his ways. The older he is, the tougher it will be. Recognize you cannot change the past, but there is no sense in waiting any longer to start doing things right. Now is the time to begin new ways of parenting. Ask the Lord for His mercy and grace, and determine that you will lift your child by name before the throne of grace—everyday. Trust Him who is able to do exceeding abundantly above all that we might ask or think. (Ephesians 3:20)

Evaluate Your Home and Family

So, let's get started. I hope, if you are married, that both you and your spouse recognize the need for change in your home. The change needed is not to satisfy other people; instead we all need to measure our lives by what is taught in Scripture. What does the Bible say? How do we measure up? That is how you must evaluate your home and especially your parenting practices. You will want to identify specific problem areas. We have given some suggestions below. And along the way, pray and keep praying for wisdom and grace.

Consider your Christian testimony in front of the children:

- Do you have a genuine spiritual walk with the Lord?

- Do you spend time in God's Word for study and devotions?

- Do you seek first the kingdom of God and His righteousness (Matthew 6:33) in your life?

- Do you maintain consistency in the standards and disciplinary practices of your home?

- Do you always maintain self control regardless of the situation?

- Do you and your spouse maintain a united front in guiding your children?

- Do you pray faithfully for and with your family?

- Is your life marked by love, kindness, and graciousness?

Consider the standards of your home:

- Is God glorified in light of the places you go and the things you do for entertainment?

- Do you have any stated or commonly acknowledged goals for your family?

- Do the topics of conversation and the manner in which people talk honor the Lord?

- Would the clothing and appearance of your family members reflect a solid testimony for Christ?

- Do family members show love and respect for one another?

- Do the children respect parental authority?

- Do family members have and enjoy good family times?

- Does the family eat together at set times?

- Are there set times for the children to go to bed?

Consider the influences on your home and family:

- Do you faithfully attend all church services as a family?

- Do you attend a good Bible-preaching church?

- Do you sit as a family in church?

- Are the friends of family members spiritually encouraging?

- How much time do family members spend watching TV and what do they watch?

- Is the computer in a common area or in an area where one might use it inappropriately?

- Is your home free from alcohol, tobacco, and illegal drugs?

- Are the children being educated in the best setting—considering academic and spiritual needs first?

- Are there certain relatives that might have a negative influence on the children?

- What kind of music is acceptable for the family?

- What message is given by posters, plaques, and pictures in your home?

- Who cares for the children when mom and dad must be away?

- Do you endeavor to protect your children from ungodly influences?

Consider the individual family members:

- Dad should think about how he should change for the best interest of his family.

- Mom should think about how she should change for the best interest of her family.

- Dad and mom might tenderly and lovingly share how they might change together for the best interest of their family.

Consider each child individually thinking through the following:

- Does he/she profess to know the Lord?

- Are there evidences of salvation in his/her life?

- What are his/her spiritual needs?

- What areas of character development need attention? For example: love, respect, responsibility, diligence, loyalty, faithfulness, dependability, kindness, humility, honesty, resourcefulness, meekness, courage, determination, self control, reverence, or patience.

Plan for Change

You might list many other areas that need evaluation in your home and family. Do not get so detailed that you are completely overwhelmed. Realize you cannot take on every area of concern at the same time, so make a plan to help you get started. As you plan for change consider the following:

- What needs to change?

- What needs to change NOW?

- What goals can we set - short term – long term?

- How can we achieve our goals?

- How can we measure success?

Keep in mind we are after long term spiritual success, not just a quick fix. Be careful of unrealistic expectations. Remember each child is different from every other child and will respond accordingly. Don't let your home turn into a military base with a long list of new "dos" and "don'ts." Changes need to be rooted in strong conviction, but flow out of loving hearts. Team work and good communication will be a must for any degree of success. The children probably did not ask for change and may not welcome it immediately. Your words, ways, and attitudes may determine if your children will respond well.

Did I mention? Pray for wisdom and grace. Pray for each other. Pray for your children by name.

Initiate Change

Initiate change with the clear understanding that as you move along you may have to adjust your plans and procedures. That is not a problem. Let everybody know that adjustment is a possibility and, if needed, it will be done. Sometimes we can come on too strong or not strong enough. We strive to do it right, but a correction in the plan along the way is okay.

Meet with the children.
Once dad and mom agree, the children need to be part of the conversation. Both dad and mom should be together and dad should do the talking. Mom can fill in the gaps if need be.

Lay out the plan.
Explain to the children the what, whys, and wherefores of how things are going to change. Let them know the positive changes they can expect from you as parents, not just the changes that will be required of them.

Apologize—if necessary.
It may be appropriate to apologize to the children, telling them that the family has not been carefully following God's Word, and that change needs to occur. If you have been abusive in words and actions, you must commit that those kinds of things will not occur again – AND YOU MUST MAKE SURE THEY DO NOT EVER OCCUR AGAIN. Success for your family may be greatly related to dad, mom, or both—re-earning the trust and respect of the children.

Share your new family goals in general, positive terms.
Tell your children you want a home that is happier, more honoring to the Lord, better organized, with better discipline. Let them know you want more courtesy, better manners, and a loving atmosphere. Do not rehearse every detail of what needs attention in every life. Billy does not need a list of his character flaws, nor does Susie need a long list of new "dos" and "don'ts." Try to bring the children on board and ask for their input as to what might contribute to a better family life. If they catch the vision for changing the family experience, be sure to incorporate as many of their ideas as possible.

Set a time for the new beginning.
One possibility is to have your talk with the children in the evening. Set the stage for the new start to occur the following morning. The morning will be a testing time as you begin the task of changing your home life and the experience of training your children.

Careful and Prayerful Implementation

Let's be realistic. The changes needed in your home will not come quickly or easily, but by God's grace, they will come. Consider two scriptural exhortations that may be helpful:

"I can do all things through Christ which strengtheneth me." (Philippians 4:13) The Lord will enable us do the things He wants us to do. You can be sure He wants you to make the right changes, so you can depend on His enablement.

"Watch and pray, that ye enter not into temptation: the spirit indeed is willing, but the flesh is weak." (Matthew 26:41) I guarantee that as you start to make changes in your home you will be tested. Exactly how the tests will come I do not know, but before long you will feel the pressure and wonder if it is worth the effort to go through this experience. It will be worth it. Do not quit when the going gets tough. Stay steady and consistent.

Let me add a few practical warnings.

- Parental unity will be essential to success.
- Open conflict must not occur in front of the children.
- Spend a lot of time communicating away from the children, so you can talk, plan, and pray.
- Recognize that one of you is probably stricter than the other and one easier going. Be sure decisions are made behind closed doors where conflicting views can be ironed out, before giving instruction to the children.
- Do not let the children divide you.
- If you are confident your new approach is in line with Scripture, you must not compromise.
- Get godly advice from others as needed, but be sure they are basing their counsel on God's Word.

Concluding Thoughts

I am grateful that long ago the Lord convinced me that His Word is true. I stake everything in my life on the validity of the Scriptures. That trust extends to what the Bible says about the rearing and training of children. If the Bible is not true then we should just set it aside and ignore it. If it is true then we must follow it as carefully as possible. The Lord wants us to raise a godly seed (Malachi 2:15). If that is God's desire for us, than by His grace it can be done.

As a parent I have made many mistakes. I can look back and wish I had done many things better. My heart's desire, however, was to learn all I could about family life as taught in the Bible. I did not want my family to repeat the tragedies experienced in my home growing up. I am grateful God honors His Word. To the degree that we followed God's Word, He has blessed and blessed abundantly. I am grateful my children have grown up to love the Lord and that they seek to serve Him. I know you can have the same blessings.

You will fail as we failed, but keep returning to the Scriptures. Keep learning. As you learn more, put it into practice. If you need to apologize to your children, do it and press on in the love of the Lord. Whatever the past has been, you now have an opportunity to begin sowing the seed of a better family life. When we sow, we do not reap immediately, but *"in due season we shall reap, if we faint not"* (Galatians 6:9). That is why Paul wrote in that same text *"let us not be weary in well doing."* Get started today. You can do this!

Did I mention that you need to pray every day for your children, and pray for them by name and by need?

> *"Lo, children are an heritage of the LORD*
> *and the fruit of the womb is his reward.*
> *As arrows are in the hand of a mighty man;*
> *so are children of the youth." (Psalm 127:3-4)*

APPENDIX I
STEPFATHERS

STEPFATHERS

Being a dad in a step family is one of the greatest family challenges of our day. Studies estimated that one in every four children that grew up in the 1990s in the United States would eventually be in a stepfamily setting. Over 90% of those children would, statistically, live with their biological mother and a stepfather. So, if you are a stepfather, you are not alone. Consider with me some information, from a variety of sources concerning stepfamilies, to help define the challenge associated with this quickly growing position in the American home.

The step family faces unique pressures. One or both mates may have a former spouse, former in-laws, or children from a previous marriage. Most partners in these marital settings admit they had little comprehension how tough it would be to combine two families. They are apparently unprepared for the fact that the stepfamily is an unnatural social setting which will not readily yield to developing relationships with the same ease as in the natural family. In simple terms, it is a whole lot easier to develop love and patience for your biological child than for the child of another. Add to that the fact that the stepfamily is often created after the heartache and bitterness that accompanies divorce.

When all the elements are factored in, it is no surprise that serious problems often arise as couples establish stepfamily relationships and children try to respond to their new situation. It is no wonder that the second marriage often yields to these pressures and consequently fails at a much higher rate than first marriages. Take heed—to be successful as a stepfather is no easy task.

Facing the Facts

Many times a single mother seeks to remarry believing a father for her children is vitally necessary for their physical and emotional welfare. Such marriages, however, do not reproduce a normal family structure. Statistically, children in stepfamilies are found to have as many or more behavioral problems than those living in single parent homes. Up to 75% of stepchildren repeat a grade in school and those same children are 70% more likely to be expelled than children living with their natural parents. Surveys show that stepchildren struggle with loneliness and run away in disproportionately large numbers. Evidence points to the fact that they have difficulty adjusting to their new family setting. To conquer these problems will require uncommon devotion from a stepdad to his children.

No doubt most men take on the role of stepfather with high hopes of success and a strong desire to meet the needs of new family members; however, the stepfather seldom, if ever, "replaces" a child's natural father. No matter how irresponsible a biological father may have been toward his children, they will generally hold him in high esteem. As a stepfather struggles with developing the necessary balance of love and control toward his children and wrestles to define his role in guidance, care, and discipline, he can experience much frustration. Perhaps this frustration is part of the reason why children in stepfamilies are more likely to experience harsh parental discipline than their peers in the natural family setting. Obviously, such is not acceptable, but, unfortunately, is too often reality.

A wise stepfather will also realize that children are often caught in the middle of parental conflicts, fearing that love to a stepfather may be perceived as disloyalty to a biological father. Sadly, adults often foster those fears by negative words and actions.

Needless to say, the facts are not very encouraging. Thank the Lord, your family can be different, but to be successful as a stepfather, you must face some hard realities and respond to them with spiritual grace and insight.

Guidelines to Help

Whether we like it or not, the role of the stepfather will vary from family to family dependent on acceptance by the children, the involvement of the children's natural father, and other factors that are beyond the stepfather's control. The Apostle Paul learned to be content in whatsoever state he found himself (Philippians 4:11). He expressed his confidence for success with these words: *"I can do all things through Christ which strengtheneth me"* (Philippians 4:13). A stepfather must find contentment with his circumstances and determine by faith to do all things through Christ as the source of his strength.

The first priority in facing any spiritual challenge is one's personal walk with the Lord. Every family will face many pressures which will require spiritual wisdom to endure. A stepfather must provide true spiritual leadership. Church involvement, prayer, devotional time, and a spiritual response to difficult situations is essential. If you as a stepfather succumb to the pressures and end up in spiritual defeat and discouragement, the family will fall when you fall. Your family must be able to see Christ in you. Colossians 2:6-7 states, *"As ye have therefore received Christ Jesus the Lord, so walk ye in him: Rooted and built up in him, and stablished in the faith, as ye have been taught, abounding therein with thanksgiving."* In simple terms, you need to be a strong and growing Christian. Pressures either drive us to the Lord or drive us away from Him. You need to make sure they drive you to Him.

To handle difficult situations in the wisdom of the flesh will usually make things worse than when they started. When searching the Scriptures and praying, we will find the answers we need for the challenge at hand. It is not enough, however, to simply open the Bible during a crisis and hope the solution will jump off the page at us. Spiritual wisdom comes through consistent and continual study of the Word of God. Gradually, wisdom is developed and the principles of Scripture are built into our lives. There are no shortcuts to maturity. Start today and receive the rich dividends in the days ahead.

The second priority in life for a married man is to strengthen his marriage. Marriages established with the best of circumstances are shaken by the storms of life. A stepfather must commit himself to being the best husband he can be. Your marriage may be a second try for you or your wife, or maybe both. If so, a tremendous amount of spiritual and emotional baggage has been brought into your relationship that may take a heavy toll on you. You will need to go the second mile in communication, tenderness, and understanding. You will have to fight off selfishness and its companion self-pity, especially when you feel you are giving and giving in your marriage, but never seem to get much in return. The challenge, to love your wife as Christ loved the Church, is one that you must heed daily. That love is best understood as the sacrifice of oneself for another (Ephesians 5:25). That is your primary marital responsibility. You will have to work hard to develop and keep a close relationship with your wife.

Usually when a young couple gets married, they have a couple of years without children. This gives them time to get to know each other more fully and work through the needed adjustments to get the marriage on a good foundation. As a stepfather you were not afforded that benefit. Consequently, the earliest months of your marriage included one or more children to fit into the adjustment period.

Whatever the particulars of your situation may be, you will need a love that can only be produced by the Holy Spirit of God, in order to give and give and give again. Remember, though, there are no other options. Your family must be a success.

Though it may be difficult, recognize as we mentioned earlier, you are probably not going to "replace" the natural father of your stepchildren, especially if there has been a divorce and he is still living. Proverbs 17:6b states, *"The glory of children are their fathers."* God has secured in the hearts of children a special place for their dad. Experience demonstrates that children often maintain a loyalty to their natural father in spite of the fact that he may have failed, hurt, or even abused them.

For two years during my college days, my wife and I were house parents at a children's home. We basically had the children with us as though they were our own. On one weekend a month they were scheduled to be with their parents or parent, as the case might be. Many of these children could have been home, but they were not wanted. One set of three, two brothers and a sister, were caught in the divorce tragedy. Their parents divorced and they each re-married. In the new marriage setting, neither parent wanted the children from their first marriage, so the kids ended up in the home. There were other situations equally bizarre. The amazing fact was that all the children maintained incredible loyalty to their natural parents.

To a large degree, as you will learn personally, your role in the lives of your stepchildren will depend on their willingness to accept you. You may feed them, clothe them, and meet many of their needs without ever receiving the love and appreciation you may want and expect. You must handle this spiritually and not fall into the trap of hurt, anger, or bitterness. You may be tempted to remind the children of their father's failures, but to do so will only bring hurt to the very ones you want to help. Let their father's deeds, good or bad, speak for themselves. Accept your role with grace, work hard to earn the children's respect, and seek to have a great spiritual impact on their lives.

You must make every attempt to be involved in the lives and activities of your stepchildren. It is hard when your efforts may not seem to be appreciated, but you need to work hard to be respected and accepted. The children did not ask for their situation; their choices were made for them. The fact that stepchildren tend to feel lonely, and often run away, is a signal that some very important aspects of stepfamily relationships are generally ignored or handled poorly. A single mom often pours her life into her children. She tries to make up for the absence of their dad and sometimes gains emotional support for herself by involvement with them. The stepfather enters the family, but instead of filling the void left by the absent father, he is often perceived by the children as taking away their mother. It is true that marriage is the primary family relationship and yours will require much time and effort. At the same time, your stepchildren must see you as a loving and devoted addition to their family, not someone who is robbing them of their only source of security and stability, namely their mother. You must be a very real and supportive presence in their day to day lives and acknowledge that when you married their mother, you accepted them as a permanent part of your future.

One of the most dividing problems in the stepfamily is the discipline and training of the children. This whole realm will demand a great deal of communication and agreement between you and your spouse. The natural parent has both the right and responsibility to address these areas, but your role must be carefully established and defined. Your goal is to achieve as natural a setting as possible, because you are the head of the home. A major question is—does your wife have enough confidence in you to allow you a free hand in the care of "her" children? If she does, how will the children respond?

Many stepfathers have fared well until a crisis in a disciplinary situation. The words, "you have no right … you are not my real father," have pierced many stepfather's hearts. A very positive response of love, firmness, and encouragement will provide the best chance to establish a strong and lasting bond. The needed message to the child is the same that a biological father might give, "I love you, but you must obey." For a stepfather the difficulty is multiplied a dozen times, but success is a must.

The children may seek to drive a wedge between you and your spouse. If they succeed, the whole family will face years of heartache and turmoil. Solid agreement on standards, curfews, chore responsibilities, and disciplinary procedures will put stepfamilies far ahead of many natural families in maintaining good order in the home.

When discipline is necessary, it must be carried out in a God-honoring fashion. Remember, discipline is not merely punishment for disobedience; it is correctional with a view toward the future. It is an opportunity to teach valuable lessons and strengthen the bond between parent and child. Never let the time of discipline be reflective of the frustration you might feel toward the whole stepfamily experience.

For every child, emotional security stands out as a very important need. As a stepfather, you must seek to meet that need and be sure your presence and actions do not undermine your child's welfare. As has already been suggested, you dare not be viewed as taking the children's mother away from them, but instead, must devote yourself to being a participant in the children's lives. It is not unusual for a stepchild to threaten to run away, believing he can find a home with his "real" father or his paternal grandparents. At such times the child needs assurance of love and a statement affirming that he is wanted, already has a home, and is staying right where he is. Too often the frustrated stepfather offers to help pack the suitcase or buy the plane ticket for the move. This kind of response convinces the child that his thinking was correct—his stepfather does not really care and would rather have him out of the house.

Along the same line, and perhaps even worse, is the threat to send a child to live with someone else, if he does not shape up. These warnings are the most destructive comments that can be made to stepchildren. They convey that love is conditional and that the parent-child relationship will continue only as long as it is convenient and not too much trouble. The toughest child on the outside is too fragile on the inside to bear the hurt that accompanies such remarks.

As a stepfather you have a unique opportunity to play a special role in the life of one or more children. There is little hope that it will be an easy task and, in fact, may be characterized by unrequited love and unappreciated effort. If you pay the price of sacrificial love and fulfill your role with eternity's values in view, you may be granted the blessed privilege of salvaging from the heartache of this world, the greatest commodity on earth, a child. Surely, He who is the father of the fatherless (Psalm 68:5) will grant you mercy, strength, and help.

Some Cautions

Parental agreement in rearing one's natural children is not easy to attain for a husband and wife. To achieve it consistently and effectively in the stepfamily can be much tougher. As a stepfather you must be spiritually and emotionally prepared for the challenge. The burden will be even greater if you have children from a previous marriage that live with you, or if you and your present wife have children together.

As the husband and father of your family, you should set the standards of discipline and practice in your home. You must establish the spiritual direction of your home and keep everyone moving in that direction. To do these tasks well, you must guard against any form of favoritism in your own actions and protect your children from favoritism shown by others. Love, support, kindness, and firmness must be equally meted out to all. Material benefits as mundane as food, toys, clothing, and education must be equally available. You must strive for balance that often eludes the average natural family. To accomplish this, you may battle your own feelings or you may have to slow down a well meaning relative who wants to make up for the seeming deprivation suffered by one of the children. As with other of your obligations, this can be a tough one to carry out, and in some instances be almost impossible, because of grandparents and other relatives. It will not be an easy task, and though sometimes it is faced by the natural family, it is almost always faced by the stepfamily and with far more complications.

An area more delicate than all the rest must also be addressed. As unpleasant as it is to consider, statistics reveal that molestation and sexual abuse occur in unusually high percentages in the stepfamily. Proverbs 9:9 says, *"Give instruction to a wise man, and he will be yet wiser."* In the spirit of that verse, I share these concerns.

Sometimes problems can occur among stepchildren. A typical case might involve an older stepbrother taking advantage of a younger stepsister. The two children are not biologically related and yet find themselves in circumstances generally reserved for the natural family. Common practices of indiscretion that would mean nothing to natural siblings can lead to trouble among stepsiblings. These could include how young people might dress in the relaxed setting of the home or that stepsiblings might be often left alone when parents are working or out socially. The wise parent will be alert to these dangers without being unfairly judgmental toward their children.

More often, however, abuse is found when a stepfather misuses a stepdaughter. The situation is the same as with the siblings. In our homes, we tend to be less discreet in our actions than we would ever be in public or in the presence of people other than family. Unfortunately, lusts that would virtually never arise in a man toward his biological daughter may be stirred up toward a stepdaughter. Some will be offended at these warnings, but no one is exempt from temptation and sin. Sin is the product of the flesh (Galatians 5:18-21), and we all are still plagued with the sinful nature. Victory comes by walking in the Spirit (Galatians 5:22-23), guarding our eyes (Psalm 101:2-3), and fleeing temptation (I Corinthians 6:18). Your personal standards of purity, prudence, and discretion must be kept very high. Heeding Paul's warning in Romans 13:14 has preserved many from getting into situations where sin might occur. He said, *"But put ye on the Lord Jesus Christ, and make not provision for the flesh to fulfil the lusts thereof."* To not make provision for the flesh means to avoid those situations where there is even the slightest possibility that Satan could get us to fall. You may be one of those few stepfathers who can earn the full trust and respect of his stepchildren. Do not violate that trust, because it is very rare and precious. Beg God to establish and preserve in your home, a wholesome atmosphere of peace, happiness, and virtue.

Concluding Thoughts

It would seem logical that first marriages and natural families have a far better chance for success than second marriages and stepfamilies. When one enters a stepfamily, emotional and spiritual baggage usually comes along. All the pressures that come to bear on the natural family are increased, and all the obstacles to success are enlarged. Many fail to see the full picture and do not count the cost involved in making the stepfamily successful.

If you are in a second marriage, you have much to overcome to achieve the measure of happiness you desire. The demand for love, patience, communication, understanding, and self-sacrifice commonly required in a first marriage will be multiplied for you. It will take work and creativity to conquer the pitfalls generally encountered in the stepfamily.

Thankfully, our God is the God of all grace (I Peter 5:10) and His grace is sufficient to meet our every need (II Corinthians 12:9). Determine to be the man you must be to make your family live in peace, harmony, and the joy of the Lord. Then make it happen, one day at a time. Count the cost and be willing to pay the price of success.

Second marriages end in divorce at an amazing rate of 65%. Your marriage can be part of the 35% that make it and the far lower percentage of people that genuinely have a good marriage. Children of divorced parents are far more likely to get divorced than children who grow up with both biological parents. By God's grace and through careful adherence to the teachings of Scripture, your children can be different.

What price must be paid for success? The price will be unusual dedication to following all the Bible says about family life and unusual personal surrender to the Savior's Lordship. Dad, to a great degree, you will determine the success of your family. Face the challenge realistically and face the challenge spiritually.

APPENDIX 11
WHAT ABOUT A.D.D.?

WHAT ABOUT A.D.D.?

Section 1 of this discussion is a compilation of information taken directly from Web M.D. Medical Encyclopedia and other resources. It has been paraphrased and edited for the sake of order and clarity. Section II of this discussion will be commentary on A.D.D. and related behavioral problems from a biblical perspective.

Information from WEB M.D. Medical Encyclopedia and Other Resources

While A.D.D. (Attention Deficit Disorder) is still a very common term to describe certain behavior problems among younger children, teens and adults, the more common term is A.D.H.D. (Attention Deficit Hyperactivity Disorder). A.D.H.D. is a form of A.D.D. where the primary problem is hyperactivity rather than inattentiveness.

A.D.H.D. is defined as "a behavior disorder with symptoms that begin in early childhood and can continue into adulthood, causing difficulties at home, school, work and within the community." (It is estimated that anywhere from 3-7% of children have A.D.H.D.)

Symptoms of A.D.H.D.

Inattention — One who experiences A.D.H.D. may be unable to focus, remember or organize; may be careless and have a hard time starting and completing tasks that are boring, repetitive, or challenging.

Impulsiveness — One who experiences A.D.H.D. may act before thinking, not make sound judgments or solve problems well; may have trouble developing and maintaining personal relationships.

Hyperactivity — One who experiences A.D.H.D. may squirm, fidget, climb or run when not appropriate; may have difficulty playing with others; may talk a great deal and not be able to sit still.

Causes of A.D.H.D.
It is not clear what causes A.D.H.D. It is known that chemical balances in the brain affect temperament and behavior.

The risk of suffering from A.D.H.D. is increased when mothers drink, smoke, or use drugs during pregnancy and when the child faces stressful family situations.

Prevention of A.D.H.D.
There is no known way to prevent A.D.H.D., but it might help to avoid alcohol, drugs, and smoking during pregnancy.

Minimizing the problems of A.D.H.D.
Though A.D.H.D. is not preventable, the problems can be minimized via:

1. Good medical care and health habits during pregnancy.

2. Learning and applying good parenting skills—including setting consistent behavior limits.

3. Maximizing preschool learning by reading to children and providing new learning experiences.

4. Using nurturing techniques

   a. Frequent physical contact—touch and hold your baby as much as possible—especially during the first six months.

   b. Limit exposure to the TV.

   c. Choose age appropriate toys—especially toys that stimulate the brain—books, blocks, puzzles.

   d. Encourage child to play—sometimes alone, sometimes with you.

   e. Make sure child gets enough sleep and rest.

   f. Encourage child to eat healthy foods—limit sugar and fat.

Treatment for A.D.H.D.

There is no cure for A.D.H.D., but the symptoms can be controlled. Treatment includes the use of various medications. Some benefit can come from Socialization Training and Behavior Management.

1. Medications

    a. Antidepressants

        i. Pamelor

        ii. Aventyl

        iii. Tofranil

        iv. Wellbutrin

    b. Antihypertensives

        i. Catapres

        ii. Texex

    c. Psychostimulants

    This is the most common treatment for A.D.H.D. Treatment is based on the theory that there are chemicals in the brain which are produced by nerve cells. These chemicals are called neurotransmitters. The nerve cells send messages back and forth across the space between the cells. This process is called Synapse. Certain neurotransmitters (chemicals) are believed to play a role in mental functioning. They include Serotonin, Norepinephine, Dopamine, and Gamma – Aminobutric Acid (GABA). When the chemicals are out of balance people can experience headache, depression, or other health problems. Psychostimulants increase the synaptic activity of the neurotransmitters (chemicals)

        i. Amphetamines such as Dexedrine or Adderall

        ii. Methylphenidate

        Brand names include Ritalin, Metadate CD, Metadate ER, Methylin, Methylin ER, Ritalin LA, and Ritalin CR.

            1. Methylphenidate is a mild stimulant to the central nervous system (brain and nerves). The exact way it works is unknown. It may cause drug dependence.

            2. Overdose of Methylphenidate may produce agitation, tremors, seizures, confusion, hallucinations, sweating, headaches, fast or irregular heartbeat.

3. Serious side effects include allergic reactions of difficulty in breathing and closing of the throat, fast or irregular heartbeat, very high blood pressure, or liver damage.

4. Less serious side effects include insomnia, nervousness, drowsiness, dizziness, headache, blurred vision, tics, abdominal pain, nausea, vomiting, decreased appetite, weight loss, and slowed growth.

2. Socialization Training and Behavior Management

a. Behavior Therapy

i. Establish routine for children.

ii. Establish rules for behavior.

iii. Give rewards or consequences depending on compliance.

iv. Train in social skills.

1. Teach child to listen and engage in conversation.

2. Teach child how to enter into new group situations.

3. Teach child how to give and receive praise and criticism.

4. Teach child how to cope with frustration.

b. Behavior Management

i. Encourage good behavior through praise and rewards.

ii. Allow natural and logical consequences for bad behavior.

1. Natural consequence—Going out in cold weather without a coat naturally leads to feeling cold.

2. Logical consequences—Logical consequences are the consequences we set up to logically follow when a person breaks the rules, values, or acceptable behavior. For example, a child who throws a toy may be required to take a time out, calm down, and think about his behavior.

c. Specific help for children age 5 and younger

i. Beware of the need for routine and structure.

ii. Tell the child what you expect.

iii. Use a system of reward.

iv. Participate with your child in activities—making puzzles, etc.

d. Specific help for children ages 6-12

i. Give clear instructions.

ii. Break tasks down into simple steps.

iii. Increase reward for good behavior.

iv. Anticipate times and situations where child might misbehave.

v. Explain consequences for misbehavior.

vi. Follow through as soon as possible.

vii. Model good behavior—be patient, understanding, and calm. Avoid angry outbursts.

A.D.H.D. may be accompanied by O.D.D. or anxiety

One-third to one-half of those who have A.D.H.D. also have O.D.D. or anxiety.

1. **Anxiety**—Anxiety is an uncomfortable feeling of fear, uneasiness or concern about the future. The emotional symptoms of anxiety are:

a. Being keyed up, on edge and easily startled.

b. Excessive worry.

c. Constant sadness.

d. Reduced ability to concentrate.

e. Increased irritability or agitation.

2. **O.D.D.**—Oppositional Defiant Disorder. The symptoms are:

a. Being hostile toward parents or other authority figures.

b. Arguing about and possibly breaking rules.

c. Loss of temper.

d. Annoying others on purpose.

e. Blaming others for mistakes or misbehavior.

f. Being overly sensitive.

g. Being angry.

h. Being resentful.

i. Being vengeful.

*Symptoms must persist over six months and cause significant family problems before diagnosis can be made.

Conduct Disorder

O.D.D. can get worse and lead to Conduct Disorder. Children with Conduct Disorder may have a pattern of lying, stealing, cheating, skipping school, running away from home, harming animals, property or other people.

Responding Biblically to the Problem of A.D.D. and Related Disorders

While the Medical Community states that 3-7% of children have A.D.H.D., I have been in churches where I have been told that *7 of the 12 kids in this class are on Ritalin* and *most of the kids in our youth group are on Ritalin.* In other words, the official message is that a maximum of 7 out of every 100 children may have this problem, but overreacting medical professionals are putting large percentages of our youth population on medication, because they see many children who misbehave. The diagnosis of this problem on local levels makes this a problem of epidemic proportions. It is not unusual for a child to be more active than his peers or for one to be of a quiet nature. Such children should not be marked as having a "disorder." A large majority of children's actions and personalities fall within the normal range. They should not be quickly labeled as suffering from a chemical imbalance.

It is significant that the symptoms of A.D.D., A.D.H.D., O.D.D. and Conduct Disorder abound in our society. It is equally significant that they are the same symptoms reflective of poor training, poor discipline, and lax parenting. These symptoms have multiplied in our society as the family unit has been weakened through broken marriages, single parenting, step family relationships, and working moms. These difficult family settings have affected the discipline and training of children. We should not be surprised by growing behavioral problems among our youth.

The medical community claims that it is not clear what causes these problems. They do state rather emphatically that the problems cannot be prevented and they cannot be cured. The Christian recognizes that while certain people may have chemical imbalances, the symptoms of all these disorders are readily produced by what the Bible describes as the sinful human nature. The whole approach of the medical professionals bypasses individual responsibility—if we do not know the cause of these disorders and since they cannot be prevented or cured, we cannot hold the child responsible or accountable for his actions.

We are told these disorders can continue into adulthood. It would appear that it would be an injustice to hold these adult victims responsible for their actions. I want to ask who they think they are kidding, but unfortunately our society is swallowing this message hook, line, and sinker.

At the root of this issue is our whole view of humanity. If we are highly evolved animals, we can surrender to this whole idea that for some reason this generation, as no other, has developed mysterious chemical imbalances producing abnormal behavior and we must try to develop medications to help the victims. On the other hand, God in Heaven told us that we have been made in His image and likeness. He has also told us that we are both responsible and accountable for our actions. He has told us that we have sinful natures which will produce all the symptoms attributed to the behavioral problems we are discussing. He has told us that people need to be saved and children need to be trained and disciplined. Therein is the pathway to victory over behavioral problems.

In my years of ministry, I have met a few people with genuine chemical imbalances. What is happening today does not match these problems as they have been historically manifested. It would seem that today's theorists have taken us to new levels of humanistic philosophy to justify the collapse of respect for authority among the current generation of young people. And we better be alert, because when they reach adulthood it may only get worse.

The medical community's primary and preferred treatment for these disorders is the use of drugs. At the time of this writing, the preferred drug seems to be Methylphenidate. It is known that Methylphenidate can cause drug dependency and can produce very serious side effects. We wonder why the preferred treatment would not be training in proper behavior. The reason, of course, is that the accepted approach to these disorders treats them as "medical" problems and "mental" problems. Chemical imbalance is viewed to be the source of the problem and the introduction of drugs, as brain stimulants, is viewed as the answer to the problem. It is said that 70% of those who receive drug therapy improve. We must wonder what the long term effect of drug-induced brain stimulus will be.

What the medical community calls Socialization Training and Behavior Management is a secondary approach to treating these behavior disorders. The recommended procedures offer many good ideas which could benefit many families. Unfortunately, recommended procedures fail to include the necessity of restraint and control of children, which is foundational in biblical teaching. For some reason the word "NO" is left out and there is no conception of appropriate corporal punishment. This is no surprise because once the term "sinful" is replaced by the word "sick," the child is no longer viewed as a young person who must accept responsibility for how he acts and treats others. He is now a "patient" who needs medical treatment.

A.D.D. and other related disorders are relatively new terms. They are often used to disguise the sinful misbehavior of young people as a sickness. Since the misbehavior is sickness rather than sin, no responsibility can be assigned nor accountability required. There is only examination of the brain and possible chemical imbalance, but no consideration of the heart where foolishness and sin reside. Since the problem is viewed as sickness of the individual, little consideration exists of the impact on the child by the family that may be in turmoil or lack the training and discipline that God requires. Since the Bible holds people accountable for their actions, we hold serious reservations regarding a diagnosis that blames sin on chemical imbalance and wonder if chemical imbalance may rather be the result of sinful behavior.

Parents are running scared. Worldly philosophy has found its way into the church. The first thought that comes to mind when we see a willful or overactive child is A.D.D. STOP! I have found few (if any) situations where A.D.D. and its related disorders have shown up in a family where sound biblical parenting has been practiced. Don't panic if your child or grandchild seems to be more aggressive than the "average" child. Don't call your pediatric psychologist because your child refuses to eat or tried to hit you when you rebuked him for doing wrong. Parents should not accept these actions, but they are sinfulness not sickness.

Get serious about parenting. The first and primary obligation of parents is to find out what the Bible says and follow it carefully in dealing with children. Believe what the Bible says. Proverbs 22:6 states, *"Train up a child in the way he should go: and when he is old, he will not depart from it."* This verse is for you and your child. Some parents want to believe their case is unique. They believe what the Bible says is generally true, but their child is an exception. It is as if the Lord knew about every other child, but missed the fact that this little guy was going to be born. What He wrote in the Bible is sufficient for all others, but not this one. NO, NO, NO!. The Bible, the very Word of God, will work for you. Not all children are the same and, certainly, not all children are easy, but the end goal for every child is the same. He must be biblically-trained to get foolishness out of his heart and to get godly wisdom into his heart.

Let others believe what they will. Look at your children as gifts from God and take the charge to train them as a special assignment from the Lord. Do it His way and reap the benefits as stated in Proverbs 29:17—*"Correct thy son, and he shall give thee rest; yea, he shall give delight unto thy soul."*

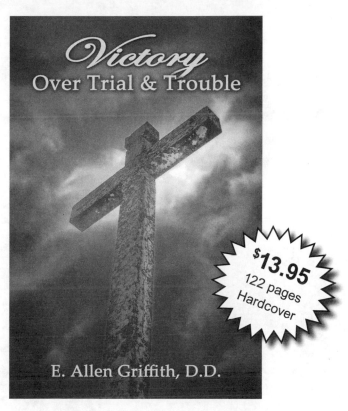

No one is exempt from trouble and heartache.
Trials are common to everyone.

During troubling times, many yield to bitterness and sorrow.
Others find spiritual and emotional victory.

What makes the difference?
Escape from defeat and self pity comes
through knowing and doing what the Bible says.

Those who really want victory can have victory.

Order your copy online at www.biblicalfamilyministries.org

ISBN 0-9749836-0-8 • Faithful Life Publishers